ENDORSEMENTS

"In this inspiring story of his search for meaning and happiness in his life, Carlos demonstrates the resilience of the human spirit. He shows the transformative power of good memories—acts of kindness, words of respect and acceptance—even when life is filled with demons of abuse, mistakes, and rejection. "The Resurrection Plant" deserves a place on high school and college English reading lists along with "I Know Why the Caged Bird Sings" and "Catcher in the Rye". This is a book to be read not only by those who are lost or "troubled young people" but also by parents, teachers, school administrators, counselors, police, and all who share responsibility for nurturing the wellbeing and potential of our children."

Nancy Schwoyer, Co-founder and President Emerita of Wellspring House Inc., Gloucester, MA

"The Resurrection Plant" serves as the perfect resource for every youth worker to learn and teach the importance of possessing intangible life skills such as purpose, hope, and self-worth in order to be able to make healthier lifestyle choices. It's a reminder that while we have no fault in what cards we are dealt in life, we are absolutely responsible for the consequences of our reactions to those barriers."

Leslie Rivera, Asst. Director of Reentry and Outreach UTEC

"Against all odds due to his challenging upbringing from the streets of Worcester, MA, to motivational speaker and now author extraordinaire, Carlos Ricard is literally living the American Dream. This book was born out of his life-long internal battles, and he has passionately chosen to share this hardship that millions of us have endured and internalized and [to show] how all of us can learn to overcome what 'appear' to be insurmountable hurdles."

John Tammaro — All Debt Solutions, President & CEO

The Resurrection Plant

Your Suffering Is Your Path To Greatness

CARLOS J. RICARD

The Resurrection Plant © 2021 by Carlos J. Ricard. All rights reserved.

Published by Author Academy Elite
PO Box 43, Powell, OH 43065
www.AuthorAcademyElite.com

All rights reserved. This book contains material protected under international and federal copyright laws and treaties. Any unauthorized reprint or use of this material is prohibited. No part of this book may be reproduced or transmitted in any form or by any means, electronic or mechanical, including photocopying, recording, or by any information storage and retrieval system, without express written permission from the author.

Identifiers:
LCCN: 2021912741
ISBN: 978-1-64746-855-2 (paperback)
ISBN: 978-1-64746-856-9 (hardback)
ISBN: 978-1-64746-857-6 (ebook)

Available in paperback, hardback, e-book, and audiobook

Some names and identifying details have been changed to protect the privacy of individuals.

Dedication

I dedicate this book to everyone who believed in me, even in times I didn't believe in myself.

CONTENTS

Prologue: Rhode Island Looks Small Until You're in a
   Police Chase xi
Introduction: Survival Is Not Your Destiny xv
The Streets, the Projects, the Ghetto, the Hood. 1
Teacher Said I Could Wind Up in Jail. 12
An American Family. 18
An Education 28
You Can't Go Home Again 36
The School of Hard Knocks 52
Gangsta University 56
How to Get Out of Prison. 68
The Glass House. 86
Trying to Take Root in Bad Soil 106
Conversation with God 119
Zig Zag Zig 134
What Goes Up—On the Streets—Must Come Down. . 141
Paying It Forward 150
Conclusion 165
Epilogue: Mom and the Birth of My Son 171
Bonus Chapter: The Resurrection Plan -
   8 Steps Towards C.H.A.N.G.E 175
About Author 177

Souls on fire come in different shapes and sizes. They come with different biographies and geographies. Although we're both souls on fire today, truly, Carlos and I grew up in different worlds. In his own words, he was born and raised in the ghetto with all the setbacks and setups that come with such an environment.

And yet, Carlos is here today, equipped with a powerful message designed to bring you greater levels of success and growth.

Carlos wrestled with this book for several years. As he wrote it, I could see a deep transformation inside him taking place. It's one thing to experience life change. It's a completely different thing to become a teacher of life change.

Through the writing process, Carlos naturally had to face his own "demons," his own past, and his own flaws. And yet, I see a different man today. He's poured his heart onto these pages because he had a greater vision for himself and a greater vision for you.

Read his words. Maybe like me you won't be able to relate to the exact details of his childhood, but don't miss this truth. We're all human and we all share a desire and a dream for something bigger than we're currently experiencing.

God Himself has implanted this desire into you. He sees the potential for greatness inside of you. And the sooner you stop running *from* Him and start running *to* Him the sooner you will find that purpose.

I know this book will inspire and encourage you. Within Carlos you will find the guide that maybe you never expected. However, this man is a fellow soul on fire.

May his words set you and your life ablaze in new and exciting ways.

—Kary Oberbrunner, author of Day Job to Dream Job, The Deeper Path, and Your Secret Name

PROLOGUE

RHODE ISLAND LOOKS SMALL UNTIL YOU'RE IN A POLICE CHASE

"Yo, we gotta stop deez pigs from followin' us, hermanito! Dey gotta go!" Felo shouted from the passenger seat.

"Put your seatbelts on, hermanitos; we bout'a go *Belly* on 'em!" Booma shouted.

I glanced out the rear window to see a small fleet of police cruisers, lights whirling and sirens blaring, giving chase behind us. Then I whipped around, put on my seatbelt, and braced myself. Beside me, Snake Eyes's face showed indescribable fear and he kept saying, "I'm screwed I'm screwed I'm screwed. I'm going to jail for the rest of my life. I'm screwed."

"Yo, put'cho seatbelt on, son!" I yelled at him, trying to snap him out of it.

"Y'all good back there?" Booma shouted.

"ADR, baby!" Felo and I shouted back, meaning *amor del rey*, meaning king love, meaning Latin Kings. Yes, those Latin Kings. But we weren't kings of anything at that moment. We were vassals of fate, kings of little more than our own arrogance.

Felo's head swiveled back and forth between the cops behind us and the interstate traffic in front of us. Doing about 90 at this point, Booma began shifting erratically from lane to lane, squeezing into any gap he could find and forcing himself into some spaces he probably shouldn't have. Suddenly, he pointed at a car on his left and yelled, "Dat ni**** right there!"

He jerked the steering wheel to the left and side-swiped a black Camry in the middle lane. The impact caused both vehicles to swerve, but both drivers brought their cars back under control.

"C'mon, bi***, spin around!" Booma pleaded. "F***ing flip or sumtin!"

I was just glad we both stayed on all four wheels. The last thing I needed on my conscience while spending the rest of my life in prison was having killed someone trying to make our reckless escape. And how much farther could it possibly be back to Massachusetts? Rhode Island always looks like such a small state, and our best chance seemed to be to get across the border where, we thought, we would be home free.

"Hit that Benz right there!" Felo said, pointing to our right.

Bang! Booma whipped the car right then quickly left again, jerking our heads back and forth with it. But his aggressive tactics weren't working. The other cars weren't spinning out and helping us escape; they were just starting to nervously pull over.

"What the f***!" Booma yelled. Hell, we probably all yelled that and more over and over for most of this ride.

"One mo time, Booma!" Felo cheered. "You got dis, hermanito! Hit dat one right there, but cum up gunnin it!"

He tried again—*crash!*

"It didn't work!"

Booma tried to turn our great escape into some kind of demolition derby, tried to turn our lives into *The Blues Brothers* or something, but this wasn't no movie.

Prologue

"All good, though," I told Booma. "They're all slamming on their breaks and slowing traffic down."

"Dey still following us?" he asked.

"One, two, three . . . damn, seven, eight, . . . *thirteen*, son!" I counted. "Thirteen pigs following us, hermanito. What the f***?"

Felo gloated maniacally, "Hahaha! Come at us, pigs!"

I narrated to Booma while he threaded through the traffic. "Dey slowed down and lined up in some type of V-formation. Haha! Dey stupid, tho. All of 'm have their lights off but this one dude at da tip. Idiot left his white light on!"

What are they really doing, though? I wondered. The cops slowed their pursuit and took up a following distance and just hung back there, watching us. The air became eerily silent beneath the growl of the engine. The weed coursing through my veins had made everything more exciting but also more confusing, more distant. But then, too: I didn't want to get too close to any of this. I didn't want to think about how bad things truly were.

Nor could I imagine that this was just the calm before the storm. That things were about to get a whole lot worse . . .

INTRODUCTION

SURVIVAL IS NOT YOUR DESTINY

I can understand how a human being could commit such a deplorable act as murder. Does that surprise you? Maybe you're already beginning to wonder just what kind of person wrote this book. Or maybe you're one of those people who has thought *I could just* kill *him!* and you think that it's not so hard to understand the capacity for murder.

Let me start by assuring you that, among my many crimes and sins, murder, thank God, is not one of them. Not that I didn't find or place myself in situations where I might have killed someone. Not that I don't know people who found or placed themselves in similar situations and actually carried through with the deed. But for whatever reason, God spared me the burden of that ultimate guilt.

Let me add that casual thoughts like *I could kill him* are not comparable to the depth of rage and indignation that energizes the actual impulse to take your hand and draw blood, the years of micro-traumas that deaden the heart to concern for others or for your own future. There's a terrible distance between the impotence of *I could kill him* and the conviction of *I'm gonna kill him.*

I understand how someone could kill someone else because I have been witness to all manner of gruesome deeds, to acts of bloody violence, to macabre scenes of mutilation and mercilessness. I've seen the reality of the asphalt jungle, and it's not the stuff of 40s noir thrillers. It's a world built on brute strength, canniness, and dumb luck. It's a world steeped in drugs, sex, booze, and blood. A world that weeds out the weak, beats out the snakes and snitches, and rewards a kind of loyalty that can end you up in jail.

I'm not proud of this. I didn't ask to see any of this, but from as early as age five my world inflicted these moments upon me. I grew up thinking I had the magical ability to be in the worst place at the worst time to see the worst things. Seeing what I saw, learning what I learned, was just par for the course. It was the information you needed to process in order to navigate the ghetto. It was the trauma you needed to experience to survive the hood. It bred fatalism, depression, abuse, self-destructive behaviors, and even suicidality. You don't survive the ghetto by being a good person, which means you don't come out much liking the person you've become.

It is not lightly that I say that by the grace of God I have overcome my past traumas and been restored from the perverse thinking that nearly led me to kill myself. And you will see that my story is not one of easy redemption but of patterns of self-destructive behavior and hard-fought battles for small and fragile successes. Not everyone I've known can say as much. Some could not escape their past and have become unrecognizable shadows of their former selves. Some are still strung out on drugs. Some live in an 8' x 12' cell. Some wound up six feet underground, their troubles over at last.

I used to think the main goal of life was just to survive it—or at least to enjoy myself before some hot head came along and ended me early. If life was a jungle, then be a big cat, strong and fierce and looking down at the rest of the food chain. If life was a desert wilderness, then be a cactus, impenetrable and durable and prickly. No one ever tells you that the big cats live in constant fear that there's a bigger cat out there, or that a human cactus is as likely to prick himself as someone else.

Introduction

There's another kind of desert plant that better describes the experience of surviving and overcoming trauma. The resurrection plant, or rose of Jericho, can survive in the desert for years without water. Its roots may detach and it will blow about the sand, apparently dead, as tumble weed. However, give it just a little bit of water and it can grow new roots and revive. Its dense leaves can even turn green again, and it can send out spores to take root and reproduce itself.

Think about that. What the world sees as a dead weed blowing in the wind is really a mother or father awaiting the moment it can fulfill its purpose. Not everyone will have the depth and volume of traumas as I have (some may even have more), but anyone can appreciate the experience of going through a drought in their lives. The resurrection plant reminds us—reminds me, at least—that mere survival is not our destiny. I believe the purpose of survival is to prepare us for our purpose.

Sure, if you're a plant, then your purpose does not extend far beyond reproduction; the analogy breaks down. For a human being, however, purpose means living *for* something, leaving a mark or a legacy. It means sending out little spores of influence that produce beautiful new seedlings that will carry forward some trace of your history.

It can be easy during the periods of drought to succumb to negative thoughts and feelings. I know as well as anyone how every part of your life can feel like a gun pointed at you, from your teachers to your "friends" to your own family. I know as well as anyone how it can seem easier to throw up your hands in defeat and become the street punk everyone takes you for already.

But I also know that as much as life can throw obstacles in your way—sometimes huge and tragic obstacles—it also gives you lucky breaks, second chances, and opportunities to take charge of our destinies. Unfortunately, we can't always see them as such in the moment, or even if we do we cannot believe it worth the risk. One of my hopes is that through telling my story I can give you the hope and encouragement you need to see those chances for what they are and to seize them. You will have to wage a constant, tiresome struggle against your own negative thinking—believe me, I know—but I'm living proof that *it is worth it*.

I wouldn't say that I'm grateful for my experiences. Like I said, I didn't ask for them and they left deep, painful wounds in my soul. But I can certainly say that every beating the world gave me helped to shape me into the resilient, adaptable, and (to the extent that I am) wise person I have become. Now that I have become a speaker, teacher, and executive and life coach, I can use my story to inspire others, planting little seedlings of myself in the hopes that I can leave the world a little greener and fresher than how I found it.

And before I get back to the narrative, let me speak to anyone who may be reading this and have hit rock bottom in their life, perhaps for the second, third, or umpteenth time: Keep in mind that nothing lasts forever—unless you want it to. Yeah, you are facing some very real problems, and a lot of them are out of your control, but if you're reading this book it means you've already overcome one of the most difficult inner obstacles: absolute despair. If you've come this far, then you are a survivor, period. And you may be curled up in a tight ball of dead leaves, but with a little bit of water you can begin to take root and open up to the world.

It's my hope that this book can be that first drop of water that gives you hope that you can become like new again.

THE STREETS, THE PROJECTS, THE GHETTO, THE HOOD

I'm pressed up against the white wall of the hallway, just around the corner from the dining room where three men sit around an old hardwood table. I'm only three or four, but I know I'm not supposed to be out of bed and I know I'm not supposed to see whatever it is those men are doing, so I'm stealing furtive glimpses of the action, half hoping they'll see me and welcome me—because I'm only three or four and like any normal toddler I don't want to be left out of the action.

The men speak loudly and laugh now and again. Sometimes in my memory they are playing cards and other times dominoes and other times they're just standing there, talking, generally having a good time. The one in the middle sports a mustache and a huge, puffy afro that, years later, I would unconsciously try to imitate.

One thing I'm sure of is that they keep passing around this key. One would take it, pick something up off the table, hold it under his nose, and then he'd pass it to the next guy. I'd never seen anyone do that with a key, and it intrigues me. But they pay me no mind, if they even notice.

The TV is on in the living room, as is the lamp, and the balcony door was open so the street light shone in. I sneak into the living room, walked around the coffee table, then back down the hallway to the bedroom. I do it again and again, taking these quick laps around the house, stopping to peek at the men until, at last, the man with the afro sees me.

He calls me over and sits me on his lap, then begins to ask me questions. Everyone laughs at my answers, and then, because I never could sit still, even as an infant, I hop off his lap and resume my course around the house.

The TV is on in my room, too. It was one way my mom would try to get me to stay put long enough to fall asleep. On one of my circuits, the sitcom or movie or whatever it is catches my attention and I stand there watching for a couple minutes. Loud sounds from the dining room snap me out of the trance. I can hear a chair being dragged across the floor and the sound of movement. I walk back to the dining room to see the last of the men leaving through the door and slamming it behind him. They've left their key on the table.

I want to see that key. I want to know what magical property it has that makes it different than other keys. So, once I determine they are really gone, I creep quietly over to the table and grab it. Upon inspection, it is a normal door key, except it has a couple spots of some white residue. I figure the best way to understand this key is to copy what the men did with it, so I hold it up to my nose and sniff like they did. Nothing happens. I hold it up to my nose again but don't sniff this time. Still nothing happens. I'm more confused than anything, so I run back to my room.

One Big Hood

This memory used to play itself back to me at all sorts of random moments but especially when I would feel down about my life and unsure what to do next. Comparing notes with my mom, I eventually determined that this was back in Puerto Rico and that one of the men was my father, a man who would disappear from my life a short time later. The feeling of the memory is one of glimpsing the dark, mysterious, adult world where men did as they pleased and the women fawned over them, of being on the cusp of a life tinged with constant danger from sources I was only beginning to be able to imagine.

Some folks seem to have minds that can shut out the bad stuff or at least numb themselves to it. Not mine. My mind has always driven me to inquire and observe and record, and every traumatic scolding and beating I received or violence I witnessed has been seared into my memory for ready access. I now know that everybody's brain (and body) records their traumas but usually in hidden ways, so it is possible, with the benefit of hindsight, to see the availability of all my traumatic memories as an advantage when it came time to start doing the work of therapy I needed to recover, but for most of my life it felt like carrying around body bags filled with my former selves.

My brain's inability to simply stash things and forget them is also perhaps why it was so hard for me to find any real respite from the unrelenting stress of growing up on the streets or in the projects or in a ghetto—all of which individually and collectively known as "the hood." These places shaped much of my childhood mind from my infancy to the time I entered school. I do not include *home* as one of these places because home did not represent some place distinctly different from the streets. Wherever I lived, whatever crap was going down "out there" was also happening "in here," meaning there was no such thing as inside/outside. It was all one big hood.

The Rebel Child of Juncos, Puerto Rico

During that memory of my dad and his buddies sniffing cocaine, my mom must have been out at work or taking a class or something. She could have just been out with friends. It hardly matters because the question of whether she should have left me alone with those guys that night misses the point. Of course, she shouldn't have left me with them. Shoot, they wound up walking out on me, anyway.

But my mother lacked the first clue about how to nurture or care for my young life. She didn't have me because she and my father wanted to start a family and nurture a microcosm of love and stability that could turn out into the world and make it a better place. I was an unintended consequence of their laissez-faire, party lifestyle, and they were determined not to let me interfere more than I had to. There wasn't much I could do about that.

Mom grew up in a massive family in Puerto Rico, one of 14 surviving children. She had what at the time was a modest but comfortable life in the countryside, though by today's standards it would be considered rustic or third world. They were in the jungle, living in a tin shack. There was no electricity or running water for much of her childhood, and the traditional ways were often tough on kids. When she acted out, she was beaten—and she acted out *a lot*. She was known as a rebel child, prideful and petulant and physically aggressive, a warrior princess born to a humble home she never quite came to terms with.

My aunt tells me of a time when they were young and had built mud houses after a rain. They would catch lizards and use them as dolls and play house with them. One day they had a competition among the siblings to see who could make the best mud house. One of my aunts won, and my mom was furious about it. So, in revenge she snuck out of the house in the middle of the night and defecated on the offending structure. Another time they were climbing trees to get some oranges and some local boys were peeking up her skirt, so she peed on them. This was all very un-ladylike, not to mention kind of gross, and it was the kind of thing that earned her the brunt of the beatings in the family.

To this day she remains a hard woman, quick to hold grudges, slow to forgive, and terrible in revenge. If she has a beef with you, forget it. It's over with you and her. In high school, for instance, she decided she didn't like one of her cousins. For no good reason, really. She'd wait for her after school on this one bridge and beat her up just because she could. This same characteristic in her meant that she could be a great ally to have in a fight, you just never knew how long the alliance would last.

Run, and Don't Look Back

One day, my mom packed up some things and took me to the airport on a one-way trip to the States. To this day I am not entirely clear what motivated her to leave everything behind to start a new life somewhere no one could find us. I was only three, and her only real plan was to stay with some relatives in a place with a difficult name called Connecticut.

Mom's life has been one of forward momentum—run, and don't look back. She didn't tell anyone she was leaving or that she was coming. Some relatives denied us entry altogether. Others let us stay for a little while but eventually kicked us out. Having grown up with the woman, I know too well how difficult a houseguest she could be. Let's just say she doesn't take well to anyone else's rules, even if it's their home.

All this meant that for varying periods of my early life my mom and I were homeless, spending a lot of time in shelters which, to my young, bewildered mind, were stuffed with violent, hateful, and/or mentally disturbed people. One night during the winter—and New England winters were tough on a couple Puerto Rican immigrants—we were scrambling to find anything like a shelter from the cold. Mom saw a man fumbling with some keys outside a large, brick apartment complex. The building's maintenance man was bald, skinny, middle-aged, and pretty surprised to see this young woman with her raggedy son in tow. He took compassion on us and let us into a vacant apartment for the night. He found us some blankets and pillows and even some food. He may have saved our lives on that cold night, but it was his kindness that meant the most to me and planted a small kernel of hope that life could be somehow different than it was. I would collect these kernels and treasure them in the days to come.

Most of the memories from the next several years are soaked in violence and fear. There was the day we took a walk to the bodega on a peaceful summer day. From nowhere, a young woman emerged and stopped us dead in our tracks with her harsh cursing. I clung to my mother's leg as this woman screamed at her, pointing her finger in Mom's face and threating to hurt her. Then I noticed the knife. After a tense moment, Mom kicked the knife out of the girl's hand and flung herself at her. Suddenly she was on top of the would-be mugger, pounding her with her fists until some people pulled them apart. I saw what my mom was willing to do to protect me, but I had never known I might need to be protected in that way. I saw an abyss of limitless violence open at my feet, and I stared into it with a cold fear.

Another time we were staying in an apartment of some kind and my mom got into it with this skinny woman who had a hot iron in her hand. They were screaming at each other in Spanish, and the woman brandished the iron over her head and looked like she was prepared to use it. Again, my mom screamed her down, making threats of her own, while I stood paralyzed by this display of red rage.

In yet another memory, Mom had hired a neighbor girl to babysit me, probably while she went to a job somewhere. This is the kind of memory that you don't tell many people, if anyone. The neighbor girl was maybe 10 or 11 years old. Blond hair, green eyes, barely having entered puberty. We were alone in the house, and she found some opportunity to pull my pants down and put my penis in her mouth. At the time, it hardly seemed out of the ordinary—just another case of being on the wrong end of the scales of power. But that's not to say that it didn't feel wrong or that I didn't feel somehow guilty. When life beats you up over and over, you begin to think you're the common denominator, that you somehow deserve it. When you get old enough to fight back, you don't have the right tools. This event awoke me to the world of adult sexuality in the worst way possible, paved the way for an obsession with girls from an early age and an adolescence spent trying to fill a hole in my soul with as much sex as possible.

In another memory we're running down a dark hallway carrying our few possessions in black trash bags, leaving behind a dude with a bad habit of hitting anything that made him mad, and nothing made him as mad as a spirited woman like Mom. That night I sat beside her as she sighed with a heavy heart and prayed to a starry night sky, addressing some invisible or absent being she called Dios or Jesu-Cristo. It felt to me like if this Dios was out there watching over us, he must have fallen asleep on the job.

Perhaps I would not have survived if every moment was like these, though even these experiences are more than I would wish on anyone. Besides the skinny white janitor, there were other moments of peacefulness. There were singalongs in the car to salsa or merengue music coming over the radio, Mom losing herself in the sad or playful lyrics. Sometimes all I would need to feel okay with the world was for her to look back at me, smile, blow me a kiss, and say, "Te amo, Carlito!"

A Home After All

We hopped from shelter to shelter like leaves blowing in the wind, often knowing hunger. Life in a shelter can hardly be called life. You have no privacy and precious little dignity. You look around at the other people there and think, "How did they wind up here? These poor people." You never think of yourself as one of them, as like them; you're always about to find something better. It never dawns on you that everyone else is thinking the same thing. *How did that woman end up here with her boy? Those poor people.*

After a time, a Catholic shelter found us an apartment in an affordable housing project. A pair of nuns drove us there and dropped us off at the entrance with a paper bag full of groceries. We stood on the concrete steps and watched them drive away in their white van. I was scanning the area, noticing the other buildings, the trees, the cars on the street. So this was home, now. I was neither excited nor disappointed; it was just another move. My mother, however, sat down on the steps and began to sob loudly.

"*No tengo como darte algo para comer, Carlito,*" she cried. "*Ay, Dios, no sé qué hacer. Dios, por favor—¡ayúdame, Jesu-Cristo!*" I don't have any food to give you to eat, Carlito. Oh, God, I don't know what to do. God, please—help me, Jesus! I followed her gaze as she lifted her eyes to an empty blue sky.

It was a rare, raw display of emotion, and it contained all the fear and anxiety of the streets wrapped up with her confusion at being offered hope, a new chance—and she didn't know how to cook the food we'd been given.

Behind us, the door to the neighboring apartment opened and a lady peered out with a face full of compassion. Her name was Zoraida, but I would come to call her Titi Mita, Auntie Mita. Her children, José and Jeffrey, became like cousins, and Mom and Titi Mita became as close as Thelma and Louise. That day we first arrived and Titi Mita saw us sitting forlorn on the steps, she couldn't help but invite us in to have dinner with them. That small act sowed seeds of love, loyalty, and hope that would stay with me forever. Through all the horrible things that happened to me, and all the horrible things I did, the memory of that family's love assured me that I was more than the sum of my mistakes.

Charter Oak Terrace, we would later learn, were the most infamously violent projects in all of New England. Titi Mita, Jose, and Jeffrey were my only refuge from a world of gang conflict, street fighting, arguing couples, men beating up their girlfriends, and homeless people overdosing.

We had hardly any furniture. We managed to get a tiny, 12-inch TV and a second-hand coffee table to set it on. Our bed was a mattress and box spring, also second-hand, that sat on the floor in the bedroom, barely keeping us out of reach of the roaches. I remember finding Mom sitting on it one night in the dark, staring at the starry sky, tears coursing down the well-known curves of her cheeks. Some part of her, I knew, regretted leaving Puerto Rico, but another part could never go back. And yet she did not know how to take care of herself, much less a child.

"*Dios, si tú me escucha, te necesito,*" she prayed. "*Estoy perdida y no sé qué hacer. Dios, si tú me escucha, por favor, ayúdame.*" God, if you're listening, I need you. I'm lost and don't know what to do. God, if you're listening, please, help me.

I did not understand whom she spoke to, but it dawned on me that this invisible *Dios* was somehow responsible for us being where we were, had pulled us through the hell of the streets and helped us find what semblance of a home life we had. What I didn't understand is why things were still so awful.

Why, for instance, did Mom beat me all the time? Why was she always yelling at me? I'd see how Titi Mita treated her kids and the way she'd look at me when Mom demeaned me in front of everyone. I knew this was not how a mother was supposed to act. The least thing—spilling my cereal, leaving my socks on the floor—would set her off. Her brow would wrinkle, her eyes become piercing beams burning a fearful hole in my heart. It felt like the energy she had used to protect us from the streets had been turned onto me, like the rage within her needed a target, however innocent. At four years old, I was learning the art of numbing myself to the pain.

It was almost a relief when Mom, Mita, and their friend Nellie would put on dresses and puff out their hair and put on all the makeup in the house and leave a trail of perfume behind them as they headed to Latino night at the discotheque on a Friday or Saturday night. This was a sort of ritual for Puerto Rican mothers who felt their youths had been stolen by no-good men. They'd rip it up—and get tore up—and not return sometimes until dawn. Meanwhile, Jose would be in charge and we would watch TV and play until bedtime.

It was one of these nights, or early mornings, that I was awoken by voices in the parlor. I came downstairs to find a man in a tuxedo looking for all the world like Burt Reynolds sitting at the dining room table with Mom. They looked at me and smiled. "Carlito," Mom said, "este es tu papa."

Ralph had a placating influence on my mother, so the immediate impact of his being around was that I got fewer beatings. She was calmer, happier, and more motivated to make something of herself and our little family. Ralph had a dry sort of playfulness and was otherwise pretty strict. He kept me indoors more than I liked doing chores or as a punishment for one thing or another. At first, he would rough-house with me and could be affectionate. Within months, however, his obsession with discipline overrode his energy for being nice to his wife's kid and he became an emotionless authoritarian.

There was this stray chihuahua in the neighborhood that winter that, with some pleading, I convinced Mom to let come in the house once in a while on very cold nights. It was a sad, skinny thing that seemed even more out of place than we were. Ralph never liked it, though, and one night he'd had enough and threw the dog back outside. The next morning, when we came outside to go to school, the dog lay frozen

The Streets, the Projects, the Ghetto, the Hood

and lifeless on the ground in front of the house. Mom and I were shocked, but Ralph simply shoved us into the car and said nothing about it. That was Ralph. That was the kind of home he was making for me.

TEACHER SAID I COULD WIND UP IN JAIL

I can still hardly believe it happened. Ralph, Mom, and I were sitting at a small table with my first-grade teachers, Ms. Deville and Mrs. Fox, for a parent-teacher conference. I already knew Ms. Deville hated me with a passion. It's possible she didn't like kids in general, I don't know, but she definitely didn't like a kid who couldn't sit still and who didn't know when to talk and when to keep his mouth shut. It would be decades before I would recognize my school problems as ADHD; at the time, they just called me a motormouth, which, for all the teachers and staff repeated it to each other and to my face, had all the force of a diagnosis.

"Carlos is extremely intelligent and has an enormous amount of potential," Ms. Deville said, which may have been the first nice things she ever said about me—but she wasn't finished, yet. "I've never said this about a student of mine, before," she continued, "but he could become someone great and do a lot of good in the world, or he could become one of the baddest criminals you've ever seen."

"Deville" isn't her real name; it's just how I think of her because of her cruelty to me during that vulnerable period. She was a short and stalky—light skinned Hispanic woman with an 80s mullet. She was convinced I was a nasty child with nefarious intentions and who could do no good, anyway. She treated me like a demon sent to test her endurance and fortitude. She would watch me like a hawk at recess. She would threaten me, often in obscene language (as in, "You little sh*t, I know you did it!), when no one could notice.

But she knew nothing about me. She didn't know how I'd been brought up on the streets, how I'd learned to numb myself to the violence adults perpetrated on each other and on me, how her petty name-calling and arbitrary punishments taught me nothing I hadn't already learned from the world.

Mrs. Fox, on the other hand, a young, kindly white woman, became something of an ally. She couldn't stop Ms. Deville from being cruel, but she would commiserate with me, usually through silent looks, or she would comfort me with silly faces or a kind touch on the arm. Add Mrs. Fox to the short list of adults who kept me connected to goodness and hope and prevented me from becoming the supervillain the Ms. Devilles of the world expected me to be.

I had been excited to go to kindergarten. We had a Polaroid from that first day. I'm walking up the grassy hill toward an overflow trailer and looking back at Mom when she snaps the picture. I'm wearing a polo shirt, slightly faded, shorts, sneakers, and a Ninja Turtles backpack, and I'm smiling. I remember what I saw, too, what's on the other side of the picture: Mom and Ralph, lit up with a rare pride, waving goodbye to me. It's the only such memory I have, a photo representing a moment when we were just a happy family for a change.

I didn't know at the time that the deck was stacked against me. I didn't know how unusual it was to know several people who had been shot at only five years old. I didn't know that it wasn't normal for a guy to set his pit bulls on his ex-girlfriend's Shih Tzu puppy to retaliate for breaking his heart. I thought those things weren't right, but I just thought that's the way the world was. When I got to Mary J. Hooker Elementary, I encountered a whole system premised on the idea that order was normal. Quiet was normal. Sharing and waiting your turn. A whole long list of behaviors that assumed the world was a safe enough place to share with other people rather than to get yours and get out of there.

I didn't understand this new world, and it didn't understand me. It felt like the whole school wanted to wipe that first-day smile off my face. They weren't as outright cruel as Ms. Deville, but they didn't have to be. They only had to show me, in word and deed, the ways they believed I was a no account Rican with no manners and no future.

I was smart and observant. The hardships Mom and I had faced aged me more quickly than kids who had easier lives. They made me alert and attentive to my environment. Wherever I went, I was observing, recording, soaking everything in, wondering why things were as they were, untangling the complicated motivations of the people we met on the streets. By the time I got to school, I had experienced a lifetime's worth of trouble and I understood the adults around me better than they ever knew.

Because my ADHD went unrecognized and undiagnosed, however, school saw me as a troublemaker rather than a troubled kid. The approach back then was discipline, discipline, discipline. Make the kid's life unpleasant until he shapes up. Don't let him think he can get away with that nonsense. It was soul-crushing. I could be a quiet kid at home, but when I got to school I found I had a lot to say. I was curious and interested in everything, and I had a huge audience, now, to interact with. I learned so much that first year, but to the powers that were, it looked like mischief, motormouth syndrome, and "hyperactivity."

The problem was that my brain worked too fast for its own good. I couldn't restrain myself from acting on whatever impulse I felt, even if it was a good impulse. Before the teacher could finish asking us a question, I'd figured out the answer and blurted it out and started to answer the next question, which to me obviously followed from the first. Or I might get so focused on something that I wouldn't even hear the teacher give me a direction, or I'd get distracted by something interesting while we were supposed to be standing in line. It was all lumped together as disorderliness and disobedience.

They held me back a year. In kindergarten.

Mom and Ralph didn't know what to do with me, but they tried to "teach me discipline" that summer and restrict my time outdoors and my access to video games. Since they neglected to help me find alternatives, I wound up getting into actual mischief out of mere boredom. When I got back to kindergarten, I was bored again because despite their assessments I had actually learned it the first time.

I passed kindergarten and, despite Ms. Deville's persecution, performed well in first grade, too. I worked hard at it, did my best to pay attention and to pass my evaluations. I had attempted to become a model student, or at least some story-book version such as I had picked up from cartoons; people even complimented me on my improved behavior. At the end of first grade, Mrs. Fox recommended I skip directly to third grade, which would mean I would be back with my same-age peers and maybe challenged a little bit more academically. But do you think that school was interested in promoting a hyperactive, motormouth Hispanic boy? Nothing in the doing.

If my story were only a tale of woe, I might have concluded it wasn't worth it to be good. Things are never so simple, though. There were adults at school who encouraged me and believed in me; it wasn't all bad. Being denied the grade advancement discouraged me, to be sure, but I still liked school, and I managed to make second grade the best year yet.

In third grade I met another Ms. Deville. Let's call her Ms. Trunchbull. She was an average height—round build black woman with a big smile and a dark heart. Her hatred of me left psychic wounds I'm still working through. She was the epitome of arbitrary authority, accusing me of all manner of wrongdoing and subjecting me to injustice after injustice for no cause I could see other than the fact of my existence. Lost recess, lines on the board, after-school detention, even wearing a dunce hat in the corner—she pulled out all the old-school tactics.

She was just mean and no way around it. Her cruelty knew no depth. The worst, for me, was at our end-of-year party. It was a tradition of hers where everyone would bring treats and share them around and have a little fun in the classroom before school was officially out. I brought my treats to share and was as excited as everyone else to eat cake and hot dogs and play all afternoon. So what does this woman do but yank me out of my chair before the party even starts and sit me in the corner by myself. I hadn't done anything—you couldn't have gotten me to act out if my life depended on it, that party was so important to me—but there I was, isolated and forced to watch my peers enjoy themselves at the party I knew I belonged at.

The part of Mrs. Fox in this story was played by Miss Sparrow, a student teacher with a good heart. After about half an hour, I guess she couldn't bear it anymore. She put two hot dogs on a plate, grabbed a can of soda and a plastic cup full of candy and brought them over to me.

"I'm sorry you're over here," she said softly. "Are you okay?"

From across the room, Ms. Trunchbull watched her protégé's display of weakness but did not interfere. Miss Sparrow's kindness about made me cry, and I offered her a seat next to me and my second hot dog. She smiled sweetly and said, "Thank you, but I'd better not," then walked away with a furtive glance in Ms. Trunchbull's direction. Ms. Trunchbull made me wait a while longer—it might as well have been several days—but she eventually released me for the last hour of the party. If she thought I'd feel grateful to her, though, she mistook me for a more innocent child than I was. I knew she had done me wrong. Letting me go was only correcting her own mistake.

The thing about being told you're a bad kid over and over is that at some point you have to conclude that you must actually be a bad kid. Truth be told, I had some evidence in support of that thesis, though it was more of the "my own worst enemy" variety. Hard as I tried to play by the public-school conformity rulebook, I could not help but speak when I should be quiet or go off on my own thing when I was supposed to be with the group. It was the best I could do with the tools and support I had.

I spent a lot of energy trying to understand why wrong behavior often felt right to me and why I always did the right behaviors wrong. The people in power, the "good people," treated me like a problem, while the "bad kids" I sat next to outside the principal's office treated me decently. Inside, I was an adventurous, curious, big-hearted kid, but whenever that started to come out I was told to sit down and shut up, that my behavior wasn't acceptable, that I was a future criminal. It made me angry, lit a fire of rage inside that obscured from view that adventurous, big-hearted Carlos that I felt was the true me. Instead, all I could see was the fire, and it made me want to burn something. You think I'm a bad kid? Well, I'll show you . . .

AN AMERICAN FAMILY

During this time, my parents had been hard at work building a better life for us. They got steady jobs and then good jobs and started to save money. We moved out of Charter Oak Terrace to a nicer place, and then we moved again to an even nicer place. My parents started making friends with "sophisticated" people. It wasn't high society, but it was worlds away from where we'd started.

Our duplex in Hartford, Connecticut, appeared modest at first, but Ralph and Mom quickly got to work outfitting it like the pool house of a Latino pop star. Suddenly, they were comfortable inviting Ralph's family to come stay the weekend, something they'd never done before.

My room had a heated waterbed, left by the previous owners. The walls were sky blue and the ceiling black with glow-in-the-dark stars. It felt like a manifestation of a frequent daydream in which I became a bird and flew away into the approaching night. But it didn't feel like freedom. Moving into a new school district and leaving behind Jose and Jeffrey only made me feel lost and isolated. Mom and Ralph tried to ease the pain by buying me things: toys, a bike, a video game system. I had brought with us this big treasure chest we'd bought at a garage sale, and over the course of a year they filled it with Hot Wheels, action figures, water guns, and so on.

It was fun having those things, but they didn't make up for feeling like a constant disappointment to them. Nothing I ever did was good enough. Nothing I said or thought was worth listening to. They saw my moodiness as ingratitude rather than discouragement. I embarrassed them in front of their new friends with my unruliness. I was a menace at school and a plague at home.

I did what we'd learned to do on the streets and fought back. I acted out intentionally, just to spite my parents. I talked back and earned myself increasingly severe whoopin's. Being struck by your Puerto Rican mother was par for the course among my fellow Ricans. Being struck by anything in reach was not unusual, either; it was even a badge of honor. Puerto Rican mothers were fierce and not to be trifled with, but at the same time everyone knew my mother took things to another level. By the time I was nine I'd had enough, and she began to take notice.

Of course, Mom wasn't going to let some kid get the better of her—she'd fought too hard to get where she was to let anyone get the better of her. We were at my Aunt Nellie's, and Titi Mita was there, too. Mom had told me to do something—probably to get her another beer or something that she could very well have done herself—and I said I didn't want to. Then she smacked me, right there in front of everyone.

It wasn't the first time she'd smacked me by a longshot, but it was rare to be smacked like that in front of other people. There had been one other notable time, at my fifth birthday party, when she had hauled off and smacked me right in front of everyone while I stood in line to get pizza. I was upset and embarrassed to be crying but also embarrassed that she had shown everyone that side of her, that they knew what she was like. Now she had done it again, and I saw the looks of helplessness on Nellie's and Titi Mita's faces. They knew there'd be hell to pay if they tried to intervene, and I knew then that I would have to face this beast on my own.

It all happened very quickly. I suddenly needed to scare her, to show her she couldn't get to me. I held my breath and slowly lifted my face up to meet hers, staring back into her wild eyes with my own hate, breathing heavily through my nose like a dragon. I didn't know I had that kind of hate inside me, certainly not for Mom—and she hadn't known it, either. It scared her, that's for sure. She spat some threat and struck me again, but I only glared harder at her. I felt a supernatural power at seeing her panic, and I hardly felt the barrage of slaps that followed until finally she sent me to my room. Before I turned away I saw the bewildered, defeated look she gave Mita.

While my bad kid side was fighting back, my good kid became obsessed with science and popular culture. The science stuff was just for me. I ordered a telescope from a Scholastic catalog and set it up in my room, and I spent endless hours observing the faces of the moon and marveling at the colorful shimmers of gas-emitting stars. My room became a laboratory, a space station, miles away from my mother's hands.

Pop culture, especially TV, provided a window of sorts into what normal families were like. Somewhere along the line I had gotten a mini television that went with me move after move. I'd sit in my room watching *The Dick Van Dyke Show*, *Married with Children*, *X-Files*, *Law & Order*, and so on. TV worlds offered a reassuring orderliness; things always settled down and came back to normal and everyone was okay. And whether the families were well-off like the Huxtables or working class like the Connors, they all loved each other and worked to restore what was broken.

This was also the season when I joined the band to learn saxophone, started playing baseball on a team, signed up for Kung-Fu and the school chorus. If I didn't get in trouble, I'd go on choral trips to sing for admiring audiences. In fourth grade, I was narrator and lead singer for the nativity play, *Silent Night*.

But my good kid felt starved, neglected, and unwanted. Mom and Ralph acted like paying for these activities checked off all the parenting boxes. They rarely came to see me play or sing, they never expressed any pride or encouragement for what I was trying to become. It makes me sad to this day to think how far a little affirmation might have gone back then. Life at an inner-city school was tough enough with the aggressive social dynamics. Add to that continuing problems focusing in class which my teachers continued to punish rather than address, early signs of adolescent depression, and a fascination with girls reaching all the way back to kissing a cute red head under the table in kindergarten, and it's no wonder my academics started to slide—which only created more problems at school and at home. If my parents had been able to show me more love and support I may have been able to hold on to that good kid a little longer.

As it was, I reasoned that, if I can't do anything right and none of the adults with power in my life even like me, why should I work so hard to please them? Why not just do what would make me happy? I looked around and saw my cousin Jose, who was a couple years older than me, who ran with some other kids in the hood and occasionally brushed up against legit OGs. Those guys were so cool, and they were free to be themselves and do what they wanted. And some of them became the flashy ballers riding around in shiny cars with two-toned interiors and looking fresh to death.

These were not just the people my environment told me I belonged with, they were the actual people who accepted me most, who understood me most. I adopted the uniform—baggy pants, baggy shirts, expensive sneakers—the cocky walk, the lazy talk, and the hard-hitting hip-hop that was the soundtrack of the streets. I knew at the time that all these things attracted more attention to me; what I didn't realize was that I really wanted people to see my sorrow.

There was one moment when someone did finally see me, and I wish I could say it changed everything for the better. I had been somehow misbehaving in art class—I was 11 or 12 at the time—and my teacher had made me meet her after school at the principal's office. She called Mom, at work, and told her what had happened, then handed me the phone. Mom was pissed that she was getting a call from school, not to mention a call at work. She lit into me like she was trying to slap me through the phone: "*No te apure hijo de la gran pu**. ¡Lo tuyo viene cuando llegue a casa!*" Don't worry, you son of a b****. You'll get what's coming to you when I get home!

I don't know how much of that Mrs. Violet heard or understood, but when I handed her back the phone her face said, *Gotcha!* I passed through the metal detector, walked out of the school, and stood atop the stairs for a moment to consider my next steps. Before *Nick at Nite*, I would have shuffled home to face the music, but now I felt wronged. I turned toward the last place I remembered feeling any happiness: Charter Oak Terrace.

That whole afternoon and into the evening I spent bumming around with friends on the streets, and it felt for a little while something like freedom, a choice I had made for myself, at least, even if it couldn't avoid the inevitable. I tried to stay over at a couple friends' houses, but they couldn't let me, so eventually I had to go home.

It was dark, and as I approached my street I heard sirens and saw flashing red, blue, and yellow lights. I prayed it wasn't at my house. Turning the corner, I saw a K-9 unit coming toward me, and a helicopter flew overhead. A search party. And I had done it, made all this fuss over not coming home on time. I was dead meat.

A responsible child would have gone to the front door and come clean about what happened, but I wasn't a responsible child—I was a survivor, and survivors do not seek confrontation. They certainly don't walk right into a beating. So, I made a break for the huge evergreen across from our backyard and hid beneath its branches. My best hope was to hide there until everything settled down and I could creep the 150 or so feet to get in by the side door, but as the sun went down, so did the temperature. I pulled my hands inside my shirt and held my backpack in front of me to shield the wind, but eventually I couldn't take the cold.

Summoning all my courage, I somehow made it to the side door, down the long hallway that led right by the front door and to the stairs, then down the first-floor hall to my room where I put on my pjs, hopped into bed, and pretended the noise outside was all in my imagination.

Suddenly, a police officer barged into the room with a loud, barking dog, scaring me half to death. I was caught, so I played the only card I had left: stupid. She asked where I'd been, and I said, "In bed." For how long? All night, didn't nobody check? Then Mom and Ralph came in. Mom sighed with relief and wiped away tears. Ralph looked distraught and unsure how to punish me for causing all this insanity.

My abuela saved me, though. The next day, she and a couple of Mom's sisters surprised us with a visit—before I could get any beating. I got away with a long, uncomfortable conversation and a stern warning.

But my reprieve was short-lived. In truth, Mom had only bottled up her anger, as she always did, until she found the least excuse to release it. In this case, I wasn't matching her shoes quickly enough, so she clocked me one. I murmured a complaint, which she heard, and the floodgates opened. She unleashed a brutal torrent of blows, bloodying my face. After a brief respite, she ordered me to clean my room, but as I entered my room I felt a sharp pain in my back that sent me collapsing onto my bed. This was new: She had whipped me with a pleather belt with a huge gold-plated buckle. My cry of pain and my collapse did not signal that she had gone too far but rather that she was winning, so she redoubled her efforts while I tried to protect my face.

I'd had beatings before, but never one that felt this way. It wasn't just about punishing me; it was about something deeper and darker, as if hurting me, defeating me, was a way to defeat all the suffering and crap life had thrown at her. She loved me as her son, but she hated me as the force in her life that had pulled her down into a world of responsibility, poverty, violence, and, I was soon to discover, a broken marriage. I didn't understand any of that at the time, of course. I only felt that it was not my destiny to know joy or peace, that I would never have the mother I'd held out hope for.

The next day at school, it was the substitute teacher who noticed something was wrong (the *substitute*! Can you imagine?). She gently tried to coax me into talking, then offered to go out into the hallway. Maybe it was the stranger-on-a-plane phenomenon that made me agree; I might not have if it had been my normal teacher. Her kindness drew me to her, though; I needed someone to see me.

As soon as we got out into the hall I broke down crying, feeling both ashamed and grateful. I told her everything. I lifted my shirt to show her the bruises. She offered what comfort she could, then took me to the principal. At about 10 a.m., Ralph and Mom walked into the main office and right past me sitting on the bench and into the principal's office. Ralph shot me a stare like he hoped I would shrivel up and die right there. It felt like someone had dropped a billiard ball into my stomach.

They exited around noon, my mother whimpering and Ralph looking chastised. I felt both guilty and vindicated, afraid to go home but grateful that Mom was finally getting a sampling of the justice she deserved. They left, and I was sent back to class to watch the minutes tick away until the end of the day. The principal assured me that, after talking with my parents, he felt it was safe for me to go home, but I wasn't so sure.

It was a long, slow, dreadful walk home that day. When I came in the door, Mom was sitting in an old Victorian chair with her legs crossed and her eyes sharpened to spears. The anticipation of the outburst was almost worse than whatever torment she had planned for me. But instead of attacking me, she said, in Spanish, "These are the only words I'm going to say to you. I won't ever lay another finger on you again. But from this day forward, you are dead to me as a son."

You'd think I'd be crushed and hurt, but honestly I felt a profound sense of liberation, as if the burden of her love had been lifted from me. I even allowed myself a secret smirk as I turned to go up to my room.

The day my mother pronounced me dead to her came after several years of new things being born into our home. The best of them was the birth of my sister, Laura Marie Lopez, in September, 1992. I was nine and not interested in sharing the house with a new kid, but I soon got over my jealousy the more I had to care for her. Mom had me help *a lot*—Ralph wasn't going to, after all; he was too busy doing man things.

For the first time, I felt responsible for someone, an innocent, fragile life with the sweetest smile and the warmest laugh. It became my job to clothe her, feed her, do her hair, and get her to the babysitter's every morning before going to school. I came to take pride in dressing her in cute clothes and finding different ways to do her hair. She was an easy baby and toddler and one of the few lights in my life.

Around the same time, Ralph opened an auto repair/body shop/used car dealership. It had been his lifelong dream to own his own business, and it hardly mattered that it was located on the worst street in the city. Mom learned how to score fancy cars for cheap at auctions and began driving around Audis, BMWs, and Jaguars. To go from nothing to a husband, a house, and a luxury car meant Mom had won at life. She had everything she'd ever wanted.

Ralph had given it to her, so though he wasn't always the most affectionate, and could be cold and stern with me, and his mother was around more now that Laura was here, though she never liked Mom and let her know it, Mom endured it all. It was still an upgrade from the life we'd been living.

Ralph, apparently, wanted to upgrade one more thing. Shortly after he opened the shop he met a woman who was attracted to his independence and didn't weigh him down with a couple of kids and a bevy of expectations like coming home on time and not wasting all their money on junkyard salvaged cars. It didn't take too long for Mom to find out, and then she was faced with either filing for divorce or living with an emotionally detached man she had to share with another woman. She chose divorce.

The ensuing months were torture for her as her fairytale life fell apart around her. She had trusted Ralph to take care of her in all their decisions, but it turned out that everything she thought they owned conjointly was, in the eyes of the law, owned solely by Ralph. With each new revelation, it became clear that Mom had been a stepping stone for Ralph, a ticket to citizenship and to achieving the American Dream, but otherwise disposable. They fought constantly, and Ralph drew out the darkest, bloodiest parts of my mother. One day he threatened to take the house and even Laura, and Mom came at him with a knife, pinning him against the wall of our basement and holding it to his throat. She was back on the streets, grabbing at anything that would protect her and her family, consequences be damned.

Ironically, we became close again during that time. Not close like a mother and son, but close like homies. She no longer cared what others would think—her world had constricted around her, again. Instead, we were in survival mode. I was her confidant, ally, and eyes and ears around the house. I was her loyal defender and respected counselor. By that time, I was beginning to live into the gangsta mold everyone told me I had been cast from, and Mom suddenly not only accepted it but almost needed it, needed me to be a street-wise tough guy who could stand by her side as the life she'd built over the last eight years was slowly stripped away from her—and another lover replaced her like an old battery.

AN EDUCATION

After the divorce, Mom packed us up and moved us to Lowell, Massachusetts, where she had some family. I don't know why else you would move to Lowell, one of the fifteen poorest towns in the state and a breeding ground of despair and all the destructive behaviors that come with it.

We were back in the hood, and I had been crafting my gangsta persona for some years, now. It was like coming home if your home is a ring of hell. On the outside, I presented the tough guy with sagging everything and chains and loud music. On the inside, rage, depression, and insecurity threatened to overtake bright, curious Carlos. My new friends were cool but kept their distance while they felt me out. I didn't have anyone who understood me.

No one except The Wu-Tang Clan, Jay-Z., NAS, The Notorious B.I.G. East Coast hip-hop served as my manual for living the life, how to talk, how to operate, how to navigate the streets. Rap was about the streets. Its lyrics were pulled from the rubble of old tenements and the barbed wire that warned us away from vacant lots, the music had hard beats like your sneakers pounding the pavement as you ran from some trouble. When hip-hop came to the party, it shoved polite society out of the way and said, "I don't got time for your whining, I might die tonight. Let's have some fun before we go."

Then there were the movies, like *Scarface*. I mean, *of course*, *Scarface*, right? It embodied the whole myth of the outsider coming from nothing and learning how to hustle and survive until he becomes something truly great.

We didn't worry about the part where he died a lonely, drugged-out, violent death. Or rather, we thought going out in a blaze of cocaine-fueled glory at the entrance to your mansion had to be better than dying alone and scared in a run-down, roach-infested apartment. Those felt like the only two choices.

Finally, it will come as no surprise that weed played a role in this period of my youth, too. It was a way to feel good when there were no other ways to feel good. It was a cheap form of medication to wash away the depression, soothe the anxiety, douse the rage—for a few hours, anyway. Weed also quieted the chaos in my brain. It was like someone dammed a river and turned the raging rapids into a gently flowing stream. Once I came down, however, my depression would come back even stronger, and that would lead me back to marijuana in an addictive cycle.

Mom didn't like any of this, but she couldn't exactly throw stones from where she was, so instead she shipped me to Puerto Rico to live with my father for a year.

Ah, Puerto Rico. Waking up with the warm sun radiating through aluminum window shutters. Reggaeton or salsa or merengue music heard from afar. Somebody frying plantains for breakfast. It was the life.

Latin music makes you feel upbeat, like life is a dance party. The instruments are so rhythmic and vibrant, and when they blend together your hips feel like seeds in a maraca—you just have to shake them. Then you hear a high-pitched voice riding along the sound to bemoan his heartbreak with the hopeless Romanticism of my culture.

Mom raised me to love this music; it came with us everywhere we went. So, when we first went back to Puerto Rico when I was 11 it instantly felt like coming home. That was also the first time I reunited with my birth father, and I spent time with him on vacations in subsequent years. Going back for a year seemed like an extended vacation. I didn't want to leave my friends, but I didn't mind putting several thousand miles between Mom and me.

My abuela and step-mother welcomed me with a warmth I'd only ever seen at Titi Mita's house. My stepmother was a charismatic, no-nonsense Cuban immigrant who held herself and her home to high standards. Dad and I had a rougher time. It wasn't like vacation, after all, when the rules are lax and time doesn't matter so much. He still had work, and he wasn't used to having a son, let alone a strong-willed teenager (I was 14), and I wasn't used to him giving me rules. After only a couple months I moved in with my abuela a couple towns over.

I was still trying to be about that life, about the hood, and that didn't play the same in Puerto Rico, at least not at first. Eventually, I found a group of peers that would hang out in the town's main plaza and breakdance and talk and eat. We did get into a little trouble, including some beef that almost got deadly. I learned that if you want to be about that life, it wasn't enough to dress the part—you better be prepared to back it up.

It was also during this time that I took up boxing. Besides feeling like an easy target for bullies—including a cousin of mine—I was drawn to the cultural mythology of boxing. In Puerto Rico and many Latin countries, boxing is a sacred sport infused with ethnic pride and patriotic feeling. It symbolized the nation's manliness and superiority over our fellow Latin hermanos y hermanas. Boxing also proved an effective outlet for my rage and pain. For six months, I gave myself over to the sport, training hard, exercising every day, excelling beyond everyone's expectations.

The only problem was that after a match I would have a raging headache. When I finally got it checked out, it turned out I have a rare condition in which there's a gap between my brain and skull. With every punch, my brain literally rattled around in my head until it swelled up. Coach said I either had to quit or risk permanent brain damage. I had no choice. Boxing had given me a new confidence in myself, but life had reminded me that I wasn't supposed to be happy.

Projects are projects wherever you go. In Puerto Rico, they were generally I- or L-shaped compounds consisting of two- to five-story interconnected buildings. They are the primary entry point for drugs and generally each controlled by a *bichote*, or kingpin. Bichotes usually started at the bottom and worked their way up by strong-arming, killing, and/or orchestrating a coup d'état.

With drugs and poverty comes violence. For all the bloodiness I saw in the States, it was Puerto Rico that began to numb me to the horrors of blank-faced death. One night, as I was walking home along the river in a haze of fatigue from boxing, there was some commotion ahead as police and paramedics rushed to the shore. Then I saw the swollen corpse floating face down, purple all over and reeking of death. Later, we would learn the gruesome details. She was a beautiful young woman from Jersey who had come to Puerto Rico and fallen on hard times. She got addicted to drugs and turned to prostitution. The report said she had been bound and gagged, raped with barbed wire wrapped around a broken broom stick, then shot in the head and thrown off a bridge. She had floated downstream for two weeks before they found her.

Then there was the night I was taking out the trash and I saw Manota, a drug dealer, stoned out of his mind and sitting against a cement wall in the alley. Manota had taken lately to using his product rather than selling it, so he was falling behind in his payments. A man walked up to him with his hood up (though it was warm that night) and begin to exchange words. The way he walked and the fact that his hood was up was enough for me to know I needed to get out of there. By the time I entered the apartment, I heard four quick shots. I crept to the back balcony and peeked over. A bloody Manota limped along the alley and fell against a clothesline post. He screamed for help as he swung around the post two or three times, then staggered a few steps in my direction, finally falling to his knees and breathing his last. Even in the dim streetlight I could see his empty, soulless, sunken eyes.

These were people who made some bad choices and got themselves into heaps of trouble, but no one deserves to go out like that. It makes you feel like the world is a cold, heartless place to see that kind of thing. People bustling about worrying about their sales reports or their retirement plans begin to appear like automatons rather than mortal beings aware of the fragility of their lives.

Perhaps it's little wonder I grew closer to the circle of outsiders I'd met in the plaza. Together, we could face down any other guys who wanted to beef with us. Or so we thought. Things could turn ugly quick in the hood. Once, Pedro (who, as it happened, was from Jersey), got himself into some trouble with a dealer from another project. He arranged a truce meeting at a public park, so we all went with to back him up. He and the other dealer were supposed to have a one-on-one and a gentleman's handshake.

A brand-new '98 Mitsubishi Eclipse with a color-shifting Chromaflair paint job pulled into the lot and out stepped the dealer—and his local bichote. One thing led to another, and suddenly the bichote clocked Pedro clean in the face. A couple of us moved forward to defend him, but then we saw the gleam of a jet-black .45 as the bichote pulled it from his waistband. I hopped on my bike and booked it out of there, but the Eclipse gave chase. I went down one road and they cut me off. I dodged down an alley and they found me again. I heard gunshots behind me and nearly peed myself.

By the grace of God, I lost them not far from my abuela's place. I knew they wouldn't venture into the territory of another bichote without a death wish, so I was safe. Safe, however, meant hiding in the apartment for three months and fearing an attack anytime I went to school or the store. The other guys had all gotten away, too, fortunately, but they also had to go into hiding.

That was a dark, depressing time. It was never good for me to be isolated, much less scared for my life. Self-destructive thoughts beat me down constantly. *Why did this stuff always happen to me? Why had I been so stupid?*

One day, bored and shiftless, I put a classical CD in my mini boombox while alone in my room. It was called *Peer Gynt* by Edvard Grieg. It was worlds away from merengue, music from the haunted forests of Europe. It enchanted me, but "In the Hall of the Mountain King" really caught my attention. A French horn moans before bassoons begin to bounce in staccato notes over the mountainside. Cellos and horns sound, drawing me to the door of the great hall and, as more instruments join and the music grows in volume and speed, pulling me like Alice down the rabbit hole into a chaos of mystical creatures and forms. A chaos, but an ordered chaos, a musical corollary to the very movements of my disordered spirit. It began a lifelong love of the stimulating and therapeutic world of classical music.

Things eventually blew over when the bichote of my projects smoothed things out with the other guy. I was free to move around and determined not to get mixed up in anything like that ever again. Unfortunately, the people around me had no such intentions. My cousin got mixed up in a love triangle, which in Puerto Rico can turn violent fast. During this time my abuela moved us into a single-family residence she'd built after decades of saving. It just happened to be not far from the other guy in the triangle.

This guy came over one night and started shooting off his mouth. We went out to see what the fuss was—my abuela, my aunt, my cousin and his sister, and myself. My cousin said a few words as he charged toward the other guy and then the guy was screaming and holding the top of his head. My cousin held a knife with a brass-knuckle handle. The guy left, but my cousin would soon learn a lesson about bringing a knife to a fist fight.

It was about two months later. We were walking away from the plaza toward our old place when a familiar voice stopped us in our tracks. As I turned, all hell broke loose. The world slowed as adrenaline flooded my system. I heard a dull thud and saw my cousin's knees buckling under him. The spurned lover was holding a black object like a pipe or crowbar and already backing away as he hurled insults at us. Then, coward that he was, he disappeared from the scene.

I managed to catch my cousin on his way down and held his bloody head while I knelt beside him. He was too heavy to move on my own, so I yelled back toward the plaza, and things kicked into gear. A couple guys came to help me lift him up while someone else pulled a car around. We threw him in the back seat and raced to the municipal hospital a few short blocks away.

He got lucky. He got 18 stitches and four staples but no evidence of permanent damage. I, on the other hand, left feeling completely carved out by life. The aggression, harshness, anxiety, and death of the streets finally caught up with me and incapacitated me. I couldn't process it, so I had to block it off, along with all the emotions my body needed me to feel. I'd later identify this as PTSD.

When I left for Puerto Rico, I never would have guessed I'd be excited to return to the States. When it came time to return to Mom, though, I couldn't wait. The beatings and neglect were at least better than fearing for my life. But there could be no confusion about whether Mom's plan to reform me had worked. She had hoped to get me away from bad influences; instead, I had been scarred in a way that put me on a path to even greater emotional dissolution.

YOU CAN'T GO HOME AGAIN

These were the truths I knew upon returning to Lowell, Mass.

1. "It's a dog-eat-dog world" should be understood literally.
2. The powers that be have it in for me.
3. It is possible, and may be necessary, to love and hate your mother at the same time.
4. Nobody understands the real me.
5. The only things that make me feel like a human being are music, weed, and my little sister.
6. This invisible man *Dios* was watching all this and doing nothing to stop it.

All the people I knew back in Lowell suddenly appeared suspect, folks who at any moment might go off on me or might draw me into some trouble I didn't want. Outwardly, I acted genial and friendly, showed people what they wanted to see, what would reassure them that I was one of them. Inwardly, I watched them vigilantly, convinced their extroversion was as fake as my own.

Thankfully, Mom didn't have room for me in the one-bedroom apartment she shared with my sister, so I stayed with my aunt up the road. That afforded me the peace and tranquility to recalibrate myself to my new life. My identity was still a work in progress. Lacking any real male role models, I would imagine myself as the speaker of the hip-hop songs I listened to, always boastful and competitive, sometimes playful, sometimes violent. I would picture myself as the hero of the crime films I watched, living lives fueled by drugs and booze and pretty girls by the poolside.

Sometimes I would get high and open a schoolbook to some random page and start reading. I still loved science and became intrigued by history and English. I loved to learn big words and impress my friends. It was among the most calming and healing times of my life.

Cue the betrayal. Life wasn't about to let me read myself back to health, was it? To spite me, my cousins, eight and twelve years old, told my aunt I had beat them one night while babysitting them. There was no talk of allowing me to defend myself; I was on the curb that day. I had no choice but to beg Mom to let me crash on her couch.

In the wake of the divorce, Mom had become more emotionally needy than ever. She had young, attractive looks and a flirtatious personality, so she could generally attract attention to her, but it was rarely from the right sort of people. Her boyfriends mistreated her and her friends were losers who could never inspire her to want anything better for herself.

Her boyfriend at this time didn't like having me there because he couldn't just throw himself around like he was used to. He was ten years her junior, which didn't make him that much older than me, and he saw me as competition. As her man goes, so goes Mom. As he grew more impatient with me, he began to lie more and not come around so much. Mom got it into her head he was cheating on her, for which she blamed me. In fact, he was cheating on her. That's the kind of guy Mom went for, after all, and it had started months before I moved in, but there was no way she would hear that from me.

The Resurrection Plant

I lay back in the bathtub and stared at the ceiling, reviewing all the things I hated about my life. A mini boombox sat on the toilet playing dark, hardcore rap that only sank me lower into my depression. I thought about Mom hitting me at my fifth birthday party. I thought about the babysitter performing oral sex on me when I was too young to know what was going on. I thought about the Shih Tzu mauled by the pit bulls, the chihuahua frozen in the snow, the Jersey girl floating in the river, my cousin lying on the sidewalk.

I had no one to turn to, no one who understood. I prayed to my mother's God, asking for a miracle. From outside the door I heard Mom berating me to hurry up and get out. Everywhere my mind turned it saw death, death, death. Beneath the depression boiled the old, black, impotent rage. I looked at the boombox, then at the water in the tub. I let myself imagine an act I finally would not live to regret.

Dios, I whispered. *I've always tried to be good. I've only ever wanted to have a normal life, to laugh and be happy like anyone else. I've never taken advantage of anyone, never done anyone wrong. Why is my life such a living hell? I've got a job and I made honor roll. Is it too much to ask for a mom who is proud of me for that?*

Depression had its claws in me, though, clouding my thoughts and obscuring any glimmers of hope. I only saw the boombox, saw the chance to punish my mother. With wet hands, I inched it closer to the edge of the tub and balanced it there. Then I lay back again and put my foot on top of it. For the first time in my life, I felt like I controlled my destiny. I and only I would dictate what happened next.

Then something snapped. The fog parted from my thoughts and my suicidal, Romantic mood dispelled. I pushed the stereo away and broke down, crying inconsolably. I felt goosebumps rise all over my body as I considered what I'd almost done, and then I heard an authoritative voice in my head: *You have so much more to live for. You're only fifteen.*

You have so many more years of life left ahead of you. This is only temporary. This was followed by a vision of my sister's face, her regular, sweet face, though it appeared to me then as an angel's. My head fell back against the tub and, unbidden, almost uncontrollably, I exalted Dios, saying, "Thank you, Lord Jesus. Thank you, Father. Thank you for watching over me. Thank you for hearing my cries. Thank you for coming when I needed you most." I had stared death in the face, and I had discovered that God had been there with me all along.

Once you reach that point where you are prepared to surrender that fundamental desire to life, there isn't much else the forces of darkness have left to throw at you. I realized that darkness is an eternal compass pointing us to the light. It is not the absence of light but its obstruction, as a roof blocks the sun.

And the darkness was far from over. After a huge fight with Mom in which she threatened to call the police on me but I called them first on her, I wound up at my Uncle Pedro's house. They loved me and treated me well, but it was clear my presence stressed them out. They had a small home for him, his wife, and his three girls. They'd heard no end of bad things about me, and everyone knew I was only there because my mother was being impossible.

That's how, two weeks later, I wound up moving in with a girl from the hood and her parents. She dressed like the rest of us in baggy jeans, shirt, and cap, and she'd been chasing me for a while. When she heard what happened to me, she talked to her mom and, to everyone's surprise, she agreed to let me move in. I wasn't into her in the same way, but my options seemed limited. Of course, this created a new problem, because I now felt guilty for using her. She was loyal, kind, and welcoming, and certainly didn't deserve to be taken advantage of. I hated being so mercenary, and I was sure someone was going to find me out and expose me as the a**hole I was.

She was also six months pregnant with some deadbeat's kid. He had taken off when he found out about the baby, but then he got jealous when he heard about me coming round. Eventually, he came looking for me one day when I was chilling downtown with some friends after school. He came at me talking tough, his chest puffed out, and in short order we were throwing punches. Cops showed up and pulled us apart, but I was seeing red and thought they were his friends grabbing me, so I gave them a few hits, too.

Swinging at a cop trying to break up a fight is not a good choice for anyone, much less a kid who can't keep his mouth shut when he's angry. They cuffed me and brought me in for disorderly conduct and resisting arrest. My friend Felo caught wind and told my aunt, who bailed me out. Mom could not be reached.

That night and for every night of the next three months I lay beside that young woman praying to God to make some kind of change, give me some kind of chance to have a normal life. Then, in late Spring of '99 a knock on the door offered me a chance to get out.

The Wellspring House, located in Gloucester, Mass., was unlike any shelter we'd ever been to—and we'd been to a lot of shelters. In fact, Mom had been homeless again after fighting with a roommate. A social worker offered to move Mom, Laura, and me out to Wellspring, a 17th-century farmhouse converted into a homeless shelter and a host of skills training and other supports to prevent homelessness. It meant leaving the relative peacefulness of my aunt's home I had returned to for a short period of time, but I felt responsible to Laura, if nothing else.

We packed up our things in black garbage bags—you don't have luggage in the ghetto—and moved into the nicest place we'd ever lived. At 16, I was a good four years older than any other kid they'd ever admitted, and they (mercifully) gave me my own room. That first night was among the most relaxing and peaceful I'd had in years.

The next morning we met two of the founders, Nancy Schwoyer and Rosemary Haughton. Nancy spoke to everyone with a straightforward professionalism that I initially mistook as New England haughtiness. Rosemary had a straight-faced demeanor, a soft British accent, and dressed like a nun. She reminded me of a cross between Mary Poppins and Nanny McPhee. I remember thinking, *This place is nice and all, but I'm stuck out in the middle of nowhere surrounded by white people in an old-ass house run by a nun and a snob.*

I couldn't have been more wrong about those two. These weren't "white saviors" leaping in with their wealth to wipe my problems away. These were women who gave of themselves and of the resources they had to really take care of people. Their steadiness, positivity, and dogged determination to treat us with respect and dignity slowly chipped away at my cynicism and allowed me to receive the kindness they showed on a daily basis. I could spend several pages trying to describe all they did for me and my family; but the crowning event for me at the time, which illustrates these ladies' generosity, came that November, after we'd only been there five or six weeks.

Nancy had received the Boston Celtics' Heroes Among Us award, which they did at a lot of their home games to honor people who made impacts in their community. Part of the award included two second-row, half-court tickets for her and a guest. Of course, I was hoping she'd bring me just because I would have loved to go to a Celtics game, but she hardly knew me, so I wasn't about to get my hopes up. What I hadn't known was how closely she had been watching my progress at the home and at my new school.

The next morning I ran into Nancy in the kitchen grabbing her usual apple out of the fridge. I congratulated her on the award and told her she deserved it.

"Why thank you, Carlos," she said, respectable as ever. "I was wondering: would you like to accompany me to the game?"

"Umm, what?" I gasped. It felt like a trick or a test. Surely, I was at the bottom of the list of people in her life she would want to take. "Thanks, really," I said, "but I'm sure there's someone who deserves to go more than me."

"That's nonsense, Carlos," she said. "You deserve a good time as much as anyone. Would you like to go or not?"

I told her yes but thought, *Things like this don't happen to people like me.* I had never been given something for nothing, before, and part of me worried I would do something to have it taken away.

About two weeks later a limo pulled up to the shelter to take us to TD Garden Arena. This was the kind of style my boys on the street had dreamed of, and here it was happening not because I'd hustled for it but because a nice lady had made a home for people like me. The driver took us around to the players' entrance where a man in a suit greeted us and gave us a VIP tour of the court. He was friendly and informative and stopped to answer our questions as often as we asked them in between showing off championship trophies and Celtics memorabilia stretching back a half century. Then he took us to our seats just a row back from where the players themselves would sit.

We made an unlikely couple—a 60-year-old white lady and a 16-year-old Puerto Rican boy—but we were both stoked and had a blast. During halftime, the announcer called her out to center court to recognize her as a Hero Among Us, and she posed for pictures with the coaches and captains of the teams. Then she motioned for me to join her, and before I knew it I was shaking hands with my childhood idol Larry Bird (then coach of the visiting Pacers) and his protégé Reggie Miller—me, a homeless kid from the hood. Throughout everything that happened to me after that day, all the moves and jail time, all the things I've lost, I have miraculously managed to hang onto that ticket stub and the memory of that day with Nancy.

I was still riding high on that experience when I tore my ACL (anterior cruciate ligament) during a practice run before tryouts for the basketball team. They took me in for reconstructive surgery, and about a week before Christmas I was home with a heap of equipment, a couple vials of meds, crutches, and strict orders to keep my leg elevated above waist level for two weeks.

Suddenly I had to rely on Mom and others for my every need and was restricted to my room with nothing but me, myself, and my disordered thoughts to kill the time. Thankfully, I had something that could receive all the activity in my brain—a journal. But not just any journal. This was a gift I had learned to treasure more than any other.

Not long after we'd arrived, a staff member by the name of Rachel McElroy-Williams took notice of me. She was an artsy redhead who exuded life and took a genuine interest in each resident, and she must have noticed my shiftlessness and how quickly the tranquility of the home registered as boredom for a kid like me. She would ask me questions and genuinely listen, slowly building trust with me until we had regular one-on-ones in which we'd talk anything from goblins to God and she introduced me to tea with milk. She was something between a therapist and an older sister, someone who could listen and ask good questions and judiciously offer insight from her own experience.

One night she handed me a wrapped gift and told me she thought it was something I could make great use of. It was a blank, black, hardcover journal with a pencil. Inside the cover she'd written, "Carlos, you have a Gauntlet with a Gift." Underneath that it said, "If not now, When? If not you, Who?"

I thanked her, not entirely appreciating the gift's significance, but I did begin to write in it. And over the following days I learned to value the way it allowed me to externalize what was inside—even more so than talking to Rachel—and to evaluate the ups and downs of my journey as a human being. I'd write down everything, unfiltered, my innermost secrets and fears, my most authentic, unapologetic self. It allowed me to explore and enjoy the fancy words I loved to learn, and it never cared if I sounded stupid or vain or whiny or sentimental or any of that nonsense. It was a barometer of my mental health, a mirror of my soul, a promise my present made to my future.

During this same period, I was learning to see another context in a new light: school. Gloucester was a very white town. I'd only had a taste of being the sole drop of pigment in a sea of pale the previous spring when a couple teachers at Lowell High had pulled me into some honors courses. I had been trying to stay below the radar, but the fact was I was good at school, and at least some people took note.

Of course, even the most well-intentioned white kids can start to bug when a Puerto Rican with a reputation as a thug sits down in their midst. And back then, I had a way of making an entrance. Take, for instance, the meeting called by Principal Sullivan with Mom, Nancy, and me prior to me starting school. I figured this had to do with my legal troubles and living situation and was prepared to sit through a heap of procedural nonsense and tell them what they wanted to hear so they'd let me in.

But I did dress up—in the way a ghetto kid from Lowell dresses up. Big, baggy blue FUBU jeans—men's size 36 for a kid who weighed no more than a buck-forty—extra-large, bright orange ESCO T-shirt, and my super-famous neon orange Doc Martins. And don't forget the bling: a big gold necklace with a large gold charm that hung down to my itty-bitty pecked chest, gold rings on my fingers, and gold earrings. I was singing "Gangsta's Paradise" in the land of "American Pie."

I'll hand it to Mr. Sullivan: he played it cool when we met. He shook my hand and welcomed us into his office. He initially struck me as Nancy had: stern and rigid with a dash of friendly smiles. He was middle-aged, tall, a bit stocky, his black hair was combed back and over, and had rugged features and an assertive voice. Mom and I recapped our story—the parts we thought would inspire compassion and show our determination to improve our situation. Mr. Sullivan listened quietly, then sat forward and pointed to a plaque on the wall behind him that read, *No Irish Allowed*.

"Do you see that sign up there?" he asked me.

"Yes, I do," I replied.

"Do you know what it stands for?"

"Besides what it says, no, I don't."

"When my parents came to this country from Ireland, these signs were all over the place where we lived. Wherever these signs were, we couldn't enter. We weren't liked very much when we migrated to America. As a kid, I was laughed at, bullied, beat up, sworn at, and treated horribly," Mr. Sullivan explained.

"Why? I don't get it," I said. "They didn't like *Irish people* where you lived?"

He chuckled kindly. "No, they didn't. Not in the least. But look where I am now. I keep that sign up there to remind me of where my family came from and what we had to go through to overcome the challenges we faced."

"Okay. Didn't know that happened to you guys," I admitted. Then Mr. Sullivan said something more unexpected yet. He looked me in the eyes and said:

"I'm telling you this because in a way you'll probably run into some of the same situations here, through no fault of your own. I want to make the time you spend here successful; I want you to vanish in my school."

"Vanish?"

"I want you to blend in, Mr. Ricard. I want you to disappear into the crowd. I don't want you to stand out or draw any unnecessary attention to yourself. You sound like a smart and good kid. I'm going to be watching you while you're here. When I feel you're sticking out and not vanishing, I'll let you know. If there's anything you need, don't ever be afraid to ask me. Also, the JROTC teacher has approved you for the program; I think you'd do well there."

This was a lot to process, not least because the first thing he suggested I do was to lose the neon orange boots. It might be easy to misunderstand this exchange from the perspective of twenty years later; a lot has changed in how we think about difference. At the time, though, I understood Mr. Sullivan's advice was meant as one street kid to another: *Here's how you survive in this place.*

Vanishing isn't easy when you're the new kid. In fact, they assigned me several guides to show me around and explain the who's who of the school—it was like school on top of school. I didn't understand why I needed to know these kids, why they mattered in my day to day life. What I didn't realize was that they were treating me with the assumption that I would participate in the life of the school like any other student, whereas I only wanted to know who really ran things and how they ran them so I could stay out of trouble.

After a month or so of honeymoon period I wasn't quite so interesting to everyone anymore and I could actually start to vanish beneath notice. This was the moment I'd been waiting for, the moment when a person's guard goes down, even for a moment, and you see what's really going on. I knew from the hood that no one was who they represented themselves to be. Everyone acted tough, but with a little experience it was easy to separate the genuinely good and honest from the shady and untrustworthy. In the burbs, everyone acted happy, which was a mask I didn't know how to see through. Who was authentic, who was sincere, and who was just fronting and a moment away from betraying you?

Just like I had in the hood, I started to watch the social patterns. Every community has them, whether cultural or traditional or just created by a dominant personality. I observed the various cliques and their relative rigidity or fluidity, who were the celebrities on campus who could do no wrong, who went about their business quietly and who needed everyone else to know about it. It wasn't so different than the hood; it was just less direct. In the hood, if someone didn't like you they'd probably tell you to your face; in the burbs, they'd tell someone else and let it get back to you later. In the hood, the big kahuna on the block was the guy willing to back up his talk with a right hook to the side of your head; in the burbs, the big fish won competitions and awards and earned the school a good reputation.

Back then, I didn't realize that the same was true of me: I was fronting in my own way. Inside, the warm-hearted kid hoped to find real friends and to fit into this new culture. Outside, my dress, expression, and demeanor said, *Stay the hell away from me.* Thus, I wound up hanging around with the loners and "weirdos," the kids who bonded over a shared contempt for everyone else's phoniness. We reveled in our difference from the in-crowd until it became impossible for us to become more than the neglected outsiders we already were.

I guess I was blending in, though maybe not in the way Mr. Sullivan had hoped. In fact, my particular brand of blending in irked me. I didn't ditch the colorful look or the gold chains, but I didn't tell anyone that I was homeless. I earned some respect among the kids who were into hip-hop, but when they invited me to their parties I had to decline because of the house rules at Wellspring. In other words, I was so close to truly belonging, but I still hid part of myself from them.

Eventually, a spark went off inside me. An overwhelming desire to have my presence among these people mean something, to leave some mark, took hold of me. Around that time, my English teacher, Mrs. Daley, noticed my interest in big words and encouraged me to journal my thoughts. It was the encouragement I needed to go back to Rachel's gift and see it not just as a dumping ground for the thoughts storming around in my head but as a tool for recording, thinking, and expressing something to an audience beyond myself.

I wrote reflections. I wrote poetry. I wrote verbose essays on any and all topics that interested me. I worked out a point of view on all the forces working for and against me. I wrote darker thoughts than I knew I had and recorded unprocessed events from the past that I could not stop to reflect upon. And then I had an idea: I would write a letter. To my classmates. Something I could read to them the day I said goodbye to them.

I rattled off a draft. I wanted to make sure I wasn't about to unintentionally stir up trouble or had perhaps revealed too much, so I showed it to Rachel, Mrs. Daley, and my honor's science teacher. They were all touched and encouraged me to move ahead with my plan. It must have been one of them that contacted the local paper, which wanted to print my letter along with a story about my family and homelessness in the region. A Ms. McCarthy came out to interview me, and we did a photoshoot at Wellspring House and at Gloucester High. The *Boston Globe* picked it up, too, and also came out to interview us. Mom was ambivalent; she worried about her friends and family learning we were homeless. I thought about the good it could do for people to hear our story, and Nancy somehow managed to support us both, but nothing came of it.

Here is the letter:

A Letter to GHS students
By Carlos Ricard

How's everyone doing without me? I know you miss me (chill, it's just a joke). I'm writing this letter to tell you a little secret I've been hiding from you. During the time I was with you, I was asked, "Where do you live? Why do you do this or that?" My answer to your questions was always false or unspecified. For a reason.

All this time we've been in school together, joked together, you've been sharing it with a homeless person. Yes, homeless. I can imagine the looks on your faces right now; you can't believe I'm homeless. Neither could I, when it first happened.

There's a wonderful place in Gloucester that helps families in need called Wellspring House. It's a shelter for families who, going through a rough time, can't afford life's expenses. It's a place for parents who for different reasons don't have a home anymore and can't afford the basics. Wellspring House helps families get back on their feet.

What a shock, huh? The kid who had a matching pair of boots for every shirt was homeless, living in a shelter. Today's society has taught us to think that homeless people are bums or drug abusers. In reality, anyone could be homeless. I know.

Before coming here, I thought of the risks of inequality I'd face going to school. Being Hispanic and coming from a place where the way people talk and dress is different would set me apart. I'd be the different one. This contributed to the vague way I answered questions and why I hid my secret of being homeless. I already had a lot to deal with, a lot going against me.

Some people look at you and treat you according to race and dress code. I've come across people who do this, only later to stand corrected when they opened up conversation with me. I know you can't say this yourselves because either you or I haven't allowed such conversation to happen. Don't think of me as "the homeless boy." I am really no different than you. As you know, I'm not like that kid or like this kid; I am the one with something new to draw the class's attention. I am Carlos.

Each of you, in your own way, has taught me something good and bad. I've come to see not everyone is the same and I try not to prejudge anymore. There were those who weren't afraid to talk with me when their friends were there. You know who you are, and I thank you. There were those who were afraid to talk to me, unsure of the response I'd give. I understand and don't blame you.

This letter isn't for you to pity me or even for you to regret anything you said to me in the past. This letter is to ask you to open your eyes, to see people for who they are and not for who they hang with, where they come from, what race they are or how they dress. This letter is for the next kid who comes to your city, your school, with my secret, homelessness.

During my time in Gloucester High School, I've hung out with people who are known as "cool" and I've hung out with people who aren't known as cool. I ask myself what is cool? Could a homeless kid be cool in your eyes? Could he have the chance to be in honor classes? Could he participate in a varsity football or basketball team with the cool kids?

Just stop a moment and think about how society has taught us to think about such things. I don't say this to everyone, only to those who do prejudge, without giving time half a chance to examine an individual.

This letter is written for that kid who is going through hard times and thinks it will never end. Don't worry, it will. There is a light at the end of the tunnel; you just have to sacrifice plenty in order to gain double.

I'm going to miss this place, in spite of what I've been through. I've learned a lot. I live my life by a quote that has helped me through this whole venture, "Good things come to those who wait."

My wait is up, and so I leave you now.

That last day of school—it was late December—I grew reflective. I soaked in the view of the ocean on the bus ride in, remembered late summer visions of the sun burning off the mist as the bridge opened to let the fishing boats through. I thought about the faces of friends, teachers, and administrators who had opened their hearts to me and for the first time in a long time inspired me to be a better person. I thought about Larry Bird and Reggie Miller. My essay published in the newspaper. How in four short months the novice gangsta who'd nearly offed himself had been chipped away by kindness and respect to reveal that the old Carlos, with a curiosity about the world and love to give it, was still inside. Something told me that God's finger, *el dedo de Dios*, was in all of this, that it was His magic at play, working through the most unexpected of people and places.

THE SCHOOL OF HARD KNOCKS

The vision of Wellspring House was that people would leave with skills and resources to help them find and keep affordable housing. Affordable housing would provide stability on which to build a life and improve one's situation. It's a vision that is part and parcel of the modern Western story that goes something like, "We're all working together to build a better society. With the right education and resources, everyone can live a better life."

The only problem is that not every community is living by the same story. Maybe in Gloucester we could have found stability and peace, but back in the hood, this time in Oxford, Mass., the story went more like, "I'm on my own. I need to protect my things, my woman, my honor, because some fool's always gonna be trying to take them from me. And if anybody gets uppity, we all gonna put him in his place. Meanwhile, we might as well live it up; we don't know how long we got."

Those two stories warred within me as I reconnected with my old Lowell crew. I had seen a different vision of the world, but I was back in a world where no one could believe in that vision—often with good reason. I had learned that, under peaceful circumstances, I could act with discipline and purpose, could excel at school and maintain positive friendships. I could sort through the thoughts in my head by writing them down in Rachel's journal. I could live a normal life, the life kids lived on TV. But now we were back in the old normal, and Mom quickly slid back into her old patterns: violent outburst, self-destructive behaviors, abusive boyfriends.

People use the phrase "school of hard knocks" as a kind of joke meaning, "I had some things happen to me and I made some mistakes, but here I am, a success." In the hood, it's no joke. It means, "Every time I get two feet under me something comes up and kneecaps me." I'd gone from my own room in a farmhouse to trapped in a duplex apartment with a raging mother. I returned to Oxford with every intention of continuing on the path I'd begun on at Wellspring. I wanted to improve my vocabulary, become known for the thoughtfulness of the words that came from my mouth. But I was back in the old school, the school of knocking you down. The climb out of the ghetto is not a straight ascent but a series of small victories inevitably wiped away by painful falls back to the bottom, and I hadn't bottomed out yet.

Trouble started quickly at Oxford High. One day I was standing in line for the snack counter at lunch when some buzzcut redneck with a whiskery pubescent mustache decided he didn't like me.

"What the f*** you looking at?" I heard him say. I had to turn around to see who said it, so I knew he wasn't talking to me. Except he was. "Yeah, I'm talking to you," he said. "What the f*** are you looking at?"

Now he adopted that stone-cold look I was too familiar with, the one that said, *Come on, just try me*. Frankly, his arbitrary antagonism surprised me too much to really be afraid, though my reflexes had kicked in such that I was already assessing the situation. I switched my cane to my right hand (yeah, I'd added a wooden cane to my ensemble at this point and used to walk with a cocky limp, to boot) and leaned toward him with an amused smile on my face.

"Are you talking to me?" I asked him. It was his last chance to shrug it off and avoid a whooping.

But this guy wasn't smart enough for that. "Yeah, I'm f*****g talking to you?" he spat. "What are you gonna do about it?"

A switch flipped in me, turning off good Carlos and waking up street Carlos. This guy might be big stuff to the other kids there, but he wasn't going to get away with this kind of thing with me.

Gentleman that I was, I squared off with him, face-to-face. "Let's do this," I said.

It was over in mere seconds. We crouched like wolves about to duel, and just as I saw a chance to catch him upside his dumb blonde head with my cane, I felt the beefy arm of our gym teacher grab my hand and drag me away. He hauled us both to the principal's where we were each given a three-day suspension.

This event showed me that I wasn't in Kansas, a.k.a. Gloucester, anymore. Oxford was a small, mostly white, blue-collar town where everyone felt proud of the hard work they'd put in to earn the barely middle-class lives they lived. Yet, to their south was a town already struggling with an opioid abuse problem, and since the drugs from Worcester had to pass through Oxford to get down there, they became guilty by association. When a brown-skinned, dope-smoking banger walks into town, it's understandable that they weren't excited to have me around; I was the epitome of the specter of drugs they worried would undermine their community. I don't blame them for that, but I can't excuse the way they expressed their fear with blatant and aggressive racism.

Besides my appearance, I was fighting an uphill battle against my reputation. Somehow the school administration and local police had reviewed my criminal record. I was a marked man. None of the administration or teachers seemed concerned that my peers would threaten me or taunt me with racial slurs. (They actually taught me a few new ones, like *sp*c*, *porch monkey*, and *wetback*, which I found more curious than hurtful as they weren't the slurs of my youth.) My JROTC commander forbade me from speaking Spanish. The principal instructed the faculty to keep an eye on me because I might be a drug dealer. This wasn't Gloucester, where they looked for potential even in their troubled students. It was more, "Let the chips fall where they may," which is to say, "Let whatever happen to the brown kid so long as *our kids* are alright."

I grew depressed again, felt isolated and outcast, and increasingly bitter. Rather than blend in, as Mr. Sullivan would have suggested, I became my own worst enemy. I wouldn't shy away from any confrontation. I wasn't afraid to back up my words with actions, and I often had to because I didn't know when to shut up. And though the "chips" always fell against me, I felt justified on an existential level. And despite the handful of white peers and their families I befriended—some of whom I remain friends with—I began to project all my outrage at this barrage of racially motivated hatred onto every white person I saw.

A handful of fellow students did commiserate with me and express their disapproval of the other students' behavior, but it would take me a long time to really connect with them. Instead, I would plot ways to get back to Lowell and see my old friends there. When summer came, I was back in Lowell every chance I got, and that's how I wound up joining the Latin Kings—but that's a story for the next chapter.

GANGSTA UNIVERSITY

"This is how we gone do this. Face and lay against the wall. Put'cho fists on your cheeks and cover your ribs with your elbows. We about to jump you in with a thirty-second beatdown to see if you got what it takes to be down with the Nation."

I stood against a wall before a group of twelve people, mostly men. The guy speaking was six-feet tall plus some, a Puerto Rican cat with a broad, swollen body like a jailhouse Vin Diesel. He went by the name King Fear, and he was the leader of the Lowell chapter of the Latin Kings & Queens.

"No blows to the face or head, right?" I asked, scared not for my safety but for how I'd look at school the next day.

"Yo, everyone, listen up! You know the rules: No blows to the face or head. Everything else is green light—kicks and everything, a'ight?" The two guys in charge of initiating me nodded and grunted.

Then he addressed me: "If you take it without asking us to stop, we'll bless you into the Nation and give you your 360s, understand?"

"Yeah, I got'chu," I said with a confident smirk.

He looked at the initiators, then at the guy in charge of the time and—according to the Nation's manifesto—formal witness to the proceedings.

"A'ight, then. Set the timer, hermanito."

You might wonder why, after all this time, after making the honor roll, after joining Nancy to meet my heroes, after tasting what an upwardly mobile life looked like—why would I still want to join a gang?

Allow me to question the question. It's the kind of people who I met in Gloucester, the people who felt they had both the right and the power to participate in society, who would ask that kind of question. Or it's the kind of family who supports their kids and whose kids can keep their stuff together in school, the kind of family who believes that hard work and the right attitude can earn them a piece of the pie.

Me? I'd had a four-month reprieve from being a criminal-in-the-making in the eyes of everyone around me, but now we were back among the old familiar structures and attitudes. The old story kicked in and pulled hard: *You're not a good kid, here, so you're either in a gang or you're a target.*

Like any institution of higher education, to go to Gangsta University you had to go through the application process. It didn't cost any money, but you had to have references on the inside, to be vouched for by them (i.e., that your ethics are up to par for the hood), and a background check to ensure you were never a rat, snake, snitch, pig, rapist, or informant. If your application was approved, you had to attend an orientation, then memorize and recite the gang's code, which would become your guiding values for life. Then there would be the hazing and initiation, after which you would be taught the club handshake and considered a full-fledged member, with all the rights and privileges appertaining, etc., including pathways to some of the world's most heavily secured institutions and severest state and federal facilities.

That's right, you'll be among the most wanted persons in town. The government itself will keep a record of all your deeds, and you'll have an opportunity for an all-expenses-paid stay at one of the thousands of state, local, or federal institutions. Graduates of Gangsta U on average rise higher in the ranks of their respective clubs, achieve higher lifetime earnings, and are just the baddest m****r f****rs around, you feel me?

I'm not bragging when I say the beatdown was nowhere near as bad as I'd been preparing for. Don't get me wrong: Ricky and Felo were the kind of guys who would punch walls for fun and could pick a man up over their heads and body slam them. Maybe they held back, or maybe it was easier to take that kind of punishment when it had a purpose other than to vent the rage of a deranged parent.

Thirty seconds later, King Fear welcomed me into the Almighty Latin King and Queen Nation, Lion Tribe. He said of all the beatdowns he'd seen, he'd never seen anyone get back up after they'd been knocked down and kicked to stay down. I took that as a badge of honor and a promise of what I could bring to the gang. We exchanged daps (handshakes) and hugs as a show of love and respect, then Fear had me kneel before him. He held up a necklace made of tiny beads, 72 sets of five alternating black and gold for a total of 360, representing the circle that was the strength of the gang together, its all-reaching power, its embrace of its members, and, unstated, its ability to identify and discipline any rats or snakes. These beads were a sacred symbol of the Nation to which I swore an oath. They were to be worn at all times and could only be removed in the privacy of my own home—or to evade detection from law enforcement.

Upon receiving the beads, I was shown the universal King salute, useful for identifying and confirming fellow Kings at home or abroad. Then King Fear recited the Five Points of the Latin King's crown, the code of honor, which I was to write down and memorize. These five points, these pillars, were what I'd been longing for—a simple, boiled down set of rules that made sense of the world. They conferred significance, membership, and identity. They guided our thoughts, words, and actions. They were a compass in a concrete sea.

Ricky and Felo became like blood brothers. We were only 16, still boys in the eyes of society, but we were done being told how to live our lives. While other kids were in their rooms listening to stories of banging women and hustling and roughing dudes up, we were living those stories out day to day. We were on a mission to make our marks on the streets as the up and coming brothas destined to become legends of the hood.

We knew we had to up our game, though. It wasn't enough to dress colorfully and talk tough; we needed some sign that we were made men. We needed to look like we'd blown-up overnight, something flashy that would blow the minds of the groupies and D-riders (the boys and girls who were easily seduced by shiny things and gangsta swag).

We needed a nice set of wheels.

For many nights we stayed up late smoking weed and working out the plan. We chose a car dealership on a busy street in New Jersey where there'd be plenty of activity to distract people from our movements until it was too late. We conscripted Booma to help. He was from down the coast a ways and had street cred for days. Four hermanitos and a bold heist in broad daylight.

The plan unfolded in two stages. On the first day, Felo and Booma wandered onto the lot and scoped the security and getaway situation while casually browsing the cars parked in the grass along the street. They inconspicuously took the keys from two Toyota 4-Runners (one white, one silver), and left to make copies. The idea was to return the originals when they reopened to not draw suspicion to the heist targets.

On day two, Ricky and I walked onto the lot with both the original and the replica keys and waited for our opportunity. We had intended to replace the original keys, but it was a good thing we didn't (a good thing, that is, in our estimation at the time), because when we finally got the signal to go and jumped in the vehicles, the copies didn't work—there was some security feature. We swapped out the replicas and used the originals to start the cars right up, and then we were barreling down the road. Moments later we were at the rendezvous, where Booma and Felo helped change the plates. After a quick fill-up, we gave each other ADR (*amor del rey*) salutes to bless the other car's safe journey back to Lowell.

For the next two glorious months, we didn't just bum around the streets looking for something to do; we rolled in high style, with heated leather seats (it was summer, but so what?), sunroof, 6-disc CD changer, and all sorts of extras such as we'd only ever dreamed of. King Fear was impressed, and our feat established a reputation for the Lion Tribe as ruthless, ambitious hustlers who would take what they wanted.

But things got hot that summer of 2000. Every week the brothers were involved in a confrontation or even a shootout with another gang. There were manhunts and territory grabs. We were riding high but the stakes were high, and the only thing keeping us from living in constant anxiety of retaliation was our steady diet of booze, weed, ecstasy, cocaine, and whatever other drugs we could kill the pain with.

When you're sitting at the top of the food chain and doped out of your mind, you can get complacent. Booma, Felo, and I were still new enough that we tried to keep our eyes open and take note of the goings on around us. We couldn't help what happened next, though. The Lowell PD came through the Chauncey projects on one of their show-of-force patrols and grew suspicious about the spiffy SUV parked outside an apartment where some brothers were chilling. They ran the plates, which of course came back stolen, then towed and impounded the vehicle. Soon after, they linked the car to the grand theft auto case in New Jersey.

Booma, Felo, and I had to hang low. We caught wind of a Hispanic Heritage Day Parade in Providence, and we figured it wouldn't be bad to get out of town. Somehow this brother named Snake Eyes joined us; he was the kind of guy who gave me a bad vibe from the moment I met him. But there we were, about to enter a real-life *Ride or Die*.

DATELINE: Saturday, August 5, 2000, approximately 1:30 a.m. EST.

THE SWAMPY MARSH WITHIN SITE OF THE MASSACHUSETTS BORDER—The trooper towered over me. Anyone would have towered over me—I was face-down in the mud with my hands cuffed behind me.

"How many of you were in the car?" he barked.

"Eighty-six, or so," I replied. He gave me two quick kicks to my face, splitting the skin behind my left ear.

"How many of you were in the f*****g car?" he barked again.

"Twelve, you f*****g pig!" I shouted back. I was grinning defiantly, which I'm sure he heard if he couldn't see. When you're this deep in stupid, it's hard to pull yourself out.

Red and blue flashers spun behind floodlights as officers from several area departments had converged on the scene to scan the scene of the crime-turned-accident for other suspects. The white 4-Runner sat nose-down in a pond, the engine still running. Booma, Felo, and Snake Eyes were long gone, so far as I knew. A helicopter could be heard approaching in the distance.

I had been manhandled, maced, thrown to the ground, kicked mercilessly, and painfully restrained. Blood and mucus flowed down my face, and black shoes passed back and forth in front of me as people shouted all around me. I wondered if this would be the time and place of my death, if my battered face would be the last image Mom would ever have of me.

Back up 12 hours and Booma is driving the remaining SUV, Felo is up front playing DJ, and Snake Eyes and I are rolling blunts in the back seat. We're all looking forward to a chill day watching a parade, getting high, and maybe finding some girls to accompany us all the while. We were entering another gang's territory, so Felo gave us the 411 on what to do if we ran into anybody.

Booma, Felo, and I had an unspoken, no-judgments, complete transparency agreement. Felo told us about the quarter pound of weed and the two fully loaded model 950 .25 caliber Beretta pistols in his backpack, which was under his seat. On the one hand, it was good to know we could protect ourselves, but on the other hand, we hadn't thought it would be that kind of day.

The day went fine until we were leaving and ran into the worst traffic. We didn't know the city or how best to reroute ourselves, and then Snake Eyes started whining that he was hungry. Snake Eyes was goofy like that, not really hardcore. Good at taking orders but with a tendency to draw unwanted attention with his destructive and unruly impulses. So, here's Snake Eyes going on about how he needs food, and us staring at taillights as far as the eye can see. At last, Booma sees a place to the left we can pull into to turn around and head back the other way—it looked like a parking lot for a two-story apartment building.

In we go, and Booma expertly manages what should have been an eight-point turnabout in just three, then pauses to make sure we're agreed on where we're going. That pause did us in. Before he could go again, a police cruiser followed by two mounted police (horses, y'all!) pulled into the lot beside us. The mounted police took up stations some distance away, to observe, I guess, while an officer from the cruiser came up to the window.

"Knock, knock, can you lower the window, sir?" he said. Booma complied.

"What's up, officer? Is there something wrong?"

"No, sir. We're just performing a standard checkup on you guys. Make sure you're not doing anything you shouldn't be. Can I see your license and registration, please?" His eyes scanned the car constantly while he spoke.

We were screwed and we all knew it. Of course we didn't have a registration for our stolen car. In addition, none of us had an active driver's license, and I was on probation after fighting the pregnant girls' baby-daddy during my homeless stint back in Lowell. Add to that the weed and guns in the back, and our only viable options were surrendering peaceably or booking it the hell out of there like the gingerbread man.

Booma told the officer he had to get the information from the glove compartment, but as he was reaching across for it he whispered to us, "We riding out like Kings, *hermanitos*." Then he put the window up and put the car in reverse. The officer overcame his momentary confusion and began to bang on the window. Time slowed down for me. It was like that scene in *RoboCop* where he scans the room to assess the threats and plan his attack. The building behind us, the cruiser to the side. Our only chance was to make for the fifteen-or-so-foot space between the horses.

Booma threw us back in drive and shifted forward. The startled horses reared and their riders grabbed on tight. Then we heard the familiar *bang, bang, bang* of gunfire.

"They shootin' at us, hermanito! Get us the f*** outta here!" Felo cried.

"Shoot the f*** back, ni**a!" Booma boomed back. Felo reached down for the backpack while Booma drove back and forth trying to break a way out. Felo found a gun and shot a couple rounds out of the window, which drew more gunfire. I could hear it puncturing the body of the car and hitting the engine. At last Booma found a side exit onto a clear street and got us on our way. The chase was on.

"Yo, we gotta stop deez pigs from following us, *hermanito*! Dey gotta go!" Felo shouted.

"Put your seatbelts on, *hermanitos*; we 'bout'a go *Belly* on'm!" Booma shouted. That's when he began ramming cars to try to cause an accident. The cops maneuvered around the traffic and made their V-formation, and for a moment we almost thought we'd make it to Massachusetts and beyond their jurisdiction. We even began to prepare our story should things still go downhill—that was part of what made the Nation so successful, our discipline in attending to details.

Suddenly, two cruisers sped past us on an overpass and disappeared over the horizon. Moments later, they were stopped about a quarter mile ahead of us, the officers standing outside their cars. As we approached, the cop on the left ran out and threw down some tire spikes. Booma swerved right and dodged them, but the cop on our right had spikes of her own, and those we couldn't avoid.

We looked behind us but could only see the officers retrieving their spikes. We pressed on, running on flats, holding onto the hope of each sign for the border. It was right there, we'd about made it, when suddenly we felt the scraping of metal on asphalt as the tires came off. The road turned, but Booma couldn't turn the car.

"The whip won't turn, yo! We going in, hermanitos! We gonna go straight for the grass. Once we do, everybody dip! Run and keep running till we all ghost. *Amor del Rey!* Love y'all, ni**as!"

We bounced and jolted off the road, through a patch of marshy grass and splashed down in a shallow pond. We jumped out and immediately sank two-feet deep in muddy swamp water. I turned to follow Felo, but the police already had their lights on us and soon enough someone had me by the shirt collar.

More hands grabbed me and I was dragged to solid ground. Then they cuffed me and maced me in the face and slammed me to the ground. I hadn't planned to make it easy as it was, but these indignities were too much. I don't know what I said, but I know I let my mouth rattle off whatever the hell it felt like saying.

"We've got ourselves a wise-guy, here," said the white cop pinning me to the ground with his combat boot.

"Oh, yeah?" said his comrade. He looked around as if to see who might be watching, then said, "Come here, you little prick!"

He knelt down over me and wrapped his right hand around my neck, pushing his thumb into my larynx as if to crush it. I instinctively tightened my neck muscles to resist him, which only made him angrier. When my neck grew tired, I put my chin down to make it harder for him to get a grip, but he just switched hands and tried again.

Eventually, he let up, but he wasn't done.

"How many were in the car with you?" he demanded.

"F*** you!" I replied.

That's when he started stomping on my face. The blows came insistently, blunt but percussive. We repeated our little comedy, him asking me a question, me mouthing off, him bloodying the underside of his boot with the side of my head. Then other officers began to arrive to coordinate the manhunt, and my buddy with the happy feet walked away as if he'd just finished a cup of coffee.

While the search progressed, any number of officers remaining on the scene found an opportunity to come by and see the spectacle of the defeated banger lying bloody in the mud. They'd laugh or taunt or sometimes just shake their heads as they circled me, but one way or another it seemed important for people to put me in my place. My indignant rage numbed me to the dozens of throbbing bruises on my head and steeled me against their smug righteousness. They couldn't do to me anything worse than I'd already experienced from someone who was supposed to be a friend—or family.

Eventually the chief arrived and brought some order to things. Officer Beat Me Up, Scotty returned and yanked me up by the cuffs, jerking my shoulders so that I screamed in agony. That made him give me a minute to get my feet under me, but he let me know what he thought of my pain by giving me another kick to the legs. Then, this state-sanctioned psycho shoved me into a trooper in front of us, who reflexively jerked around and gave me an elbow to my nose. I saw white and fell back to the ground.

At last they threw me in a cruiser and left me alone—or so I thought. Before we were on our way a black officer opened the door and asked me how I was doing. I turned to show him the hamburger where the left side of my face used to be. That's when the worthless piece of you-know-what spat right in my face and told me he'd shoot me in the head if his chief hadn't already shown up.

Some time later they had finally found everyone. Booma was the toughest: a chopper with a thermographic camera spotted him hiding underwater and breathing through a reed like a straight up ninja. They took us to the state barracks at Foxborough, Mass., where I was able to wash my face with cold water and assess the damage. As best as I could see through my swollen eyelid, my left eye was blood red. My cheek had swollen to the size of a purple, black, and blue softball, and I had a circular laceration about one inch in diameter above that. It took them three hours to send me to a hospital, and that was only when they learned I was a minor and that they could get in big trouble for beating me up. The hospital staff were visibly upset by my appearance. I got eleven stitches in my left ear and some antiseptic. An X-ray revealed a perfectly centered fracture in my nose. The police report stated that the "cuts and bruises were likely sustained upon the vehicle's high-speed impact and during the process of running through 'sticks and branches' in a heavily wooded area."

This is what justice looked like for us brown-skinned kids in the liberal enclave of New England. There's no question we were in the wrong, but tell me how anything those police did to me was supposed to teach me that the police are the good guys or that "good" means something other than "powerful"? You can call it a few bad cops, but somehow the system let those few bad cops get away with torture in the name of the good State of Massachusetts. At least the Kings told me it was coming—and stayed away from my face. Who would you pledge allegiance to?

HOW TO GET OUT OF PRISON

The following morning, a Sunday, they took me to Westboro Detention Center for Juvenile Delinquents. The staff's faces told me all I needed to know, and one guy confided that I was one of the worst cases he'd seen in 30 years. They didn't believe a word of the police report; in fact, it angered them to read what they recognized as outright lies. But the record was the record, and no one was going to win against a cop's word on hearsay or the perp's testimony, so the best they could do was to take detailed photos and put them in my record.

Monday, they took me to court, where the DA ran through a list of charges. Since I was a minor, my record is protected from public knowledge in the State of Massachusetts, so it's difficult, even for me, to get access. They clearly planned to throw the book at me and send a message that you don't shoot at cops and lead them on a high-speed chase without feeling the hurt. Among the charges I can recall were:

- Grand Larceny of a Motor Vehicle (a.k.a. Grand Theft Auto)
- Operating to Endanger (a.k.a. Reckless Operation of a Motor Vehicle)
- Possession of a Firearm (two counts)
- Illegal Discharge of a Firearm
- Resisting Arrest
- Possession of a Class B Substance (Marijuana)

It felt like a Mike Tyson punch to the gut—that ends-the-match-in-ten-seconds-after-you-spent-$50-on-Pay-Per-View kind of Mike Tyson punch. Then, while I was recovering from having the wind knocked out of me, someone pulled the rug out from under me, too. The DA read a part of one trooper's report to the effect that one Mr. Snake Eyes—a so-called brother in the Almighty Latin King & Queen Nation, Lion Tribe—not only ran off his mouth, i.e., turned snitch, but lied to boot and put *me* in the driver's seat *and* added some nonsense about us having stopped at a Burger King earlier that night.

How Snake Eyes could put his own life in danger by turning snitch was beyond me. And you know I just about lost my mind over that Burger King part—it was his damn whining about food that landed us in that spot in the first place. Not that it mattered a whole lot for the time being. The judge put my bond at $10,000, which was way beyond anything we could afford, so I was thrown into Plymouth County Correctional where I would do three months of dead time until my trial.

In one of the first strokes of good luck in my life, the court appointed me one of the best criminal trial lawyers in the state, if not New England. But if you've been paying attention up to this point, you know that didn't last. The day of an important hearing, some other case came up that was more pressing, so he handed me off to a lady who was nice and sweet and all but, besides being about 80 years old didn't know anything about my case except for the folder she'd just been handed and did not seem up to the task of being the bulldog I needed.

I hadn't wasted my time in Plymouth County, though. I'd studied the case and seen the holes in the police report and assembled my own case in my mind. During the reading of the deposition, the DA got confused for some reason and started searching through some papers. I leaned over to my attorney and began explaining some of the problems with the police report—problems it was clear she hadn't noted. Fortuitously, the judge asked my attorney if she wanted to add anything while we waited for the DA to continue.

This was one of the few times my "motormouth" actually helped me out of a situation. Impulsively, I began to speak before my counsel could, but I caught myself at, "You're Hon—" The judge gazed down at me, intrigued, and asked me to continue. I thought I'd stepped in it for sure, but I also certainly had things to say. It was time to crap or get off the pot.

Maybe God guided my words in that moment, or maybe it was the combination of irritation at the DA's nonsense and the pressure of the moment, but once I got the green light to speak, I went ahead and spoke. I walked the judge through a laundry list of inconsistencies in the DA's report. They'd gotten some of the timeline wrong, for starters, and they couldn't pin guns or marijuana on me because they were inside a backpack in the back of the vehicle. Furthermore, Booma had by this time confessed to being the driver, not me (a fact I hinted the DA should have already known). My case was simple: They could place me there in the car, but they couldn't pin any of the illegal activity on me. I didn't have to snitch on anyone or even lie; I just did not incriminate myself.

The DA had meanwhile gotten her act together and looked none too pleased to be waiting for this teenage criminal to finish picking apart her case. The judge asked if anything I said was false or inconsistent with the facts, and shockingly the DA didn't know how to respond. She said, "Yes, but the state cannot provide further details at this time." Allegedly, she couldn't find some document she needed.

The judge looked back at my attorney and me and asked me what I hoped to be when I got older.

"Be a lawyer and eventually sit where you are, Your Honor," I said, throwing in a slight smile.

She chuckled and told me I had potential and could become a judge if I'd just stay out of trouble. "And I know you can do it," she concluded. Then she announced, "The defendant is to be released on his own personal recognizance."

I was a free man, again. Not only that, but she dropped all the most serious charges. I couldn't believe it. Out in the hallway, my lawyer congratulated me and said that in her entire career (which I assumed was extensive) she'd never seen a defendant speak to a judge in so convincing a manner that it led to such a favorable outcome.

"You have a lot of potential, Carlos," she said, echoing the judge. "You are an extremely smart young man. Stay out of trouble and you could become whatever you want to be."

I'd heard those words from so many people, but that day, when it meant the difference between going (back) to prison and walking free, they really began to sink in and take root in my heart. They would have to wait there for some time, though, before they could really inspire me to blossom.

I went home to Mom and Laura and hid myself away for a couple weeks to reacclimate to society—and to avoid the inevitable questions as well as any chance of getting in trouble again. I went out on Halloween with some friends, and wouldn't you know it, some cops show up while we're just bumming around a park. One of them recognized me and said, "Say, you're the cop killer, huh? When the hell did they let *you* out?"

That was it. When I went to school the next day—my first day back of that school year—my reputation had been established. No longer the honor roll JROTC kid, I was confirmed as the cop-killing gangbanger they knew I'd always been deep down. Not surprisingly, school became more unbearable, until I stopped going altogether, found a job, and found a group of party people to kill my time with. And the good people of Oxford, Mass., checked "high-school dropout" off their Carlos the Banger bingo cards.

Thus began a period of newfound freedom and irresponsibility. With money coming in and no school to worry about, I was more my own man than I'd ever been. I built my life around the paradoxical beliefs that I was bright and full of promise and that I had no future. Because I was bright, I saw through society's hypocrisy (a cop trying to kick your head in will help with that insight, too). Because I had no future, I didn't worry too much about the consequences of my actions.

Not surprisingly, being known as the "cop killer" didn't make me popular among the local PD. They took every opportunity to harass me and threaten me and generally let me know they'd be happy to break my skull if I'd only give them a chance. By now, you know me: I just about gave it to them. Here's a sample of my arrests just from 2002:

- **05/20/2002**: Dudley PD. *Charge*: Minor in Possession of Alcohol (Misdemeanor)
- **07/03/2002**: Oxford PD. *Charge*: Minor in Possession of Alcohol (Misdemeanor)
- **08/27/2002**: Oxford PD. *Charge*: Wanton Destruction of Property (Misdemeanor)
- **09/06/2002**: Oxford PD. *Charge*: Assault W/ Dangerous Weapon (Felony). Amended to Assault (Misdemeanor). *Charge*: Breaking & Entering Night Time with Intent to Commit Felony (*Charge* Dismissed). *Charge*: Threatening to Commit Crime (Misdemeanor)

- **12/03/2002**: Auburn PD. *Charge*: Counterfeit Note in Possession (Felony; Dismissed). *Charge*: Operating After Suspension (Misdemeanor)

The street story was winning, and I wasn't putting up much of a fight. I embraced the thug image, became the kind of punk police pointed to when they tried to justify racial profiling: the gangbanger who got high every day, got into trouble every other day, and would screw anything that was a "5" or above.

I grew out an afro, which over time became cornrows in various patterns over my head. If I was really feeling hood, I'd undo half my head and pick the hell out of it until it puffed out like a Soul Train dance king. I'd become every parent's nightmare; the secret Puerto Rican fantasy of a surprising number of white girls and a pain in the ass for their brothers; a corrupting influence for black, white, and brown alike; and target for any underage redneck full of liquid muscle at a house party. I had a personal vendetta against middle-class morality, and I let everyone know it. As often as not, I'd find a compatriot to join me in whatever escapade I was up to.

Nothing made me feel as whole as being with my brothers and sisters in the Almighty King & Queen Nation. No one else shared the experiences us street kids did, and no one felt as authentic as my gang family. The irony, of course, was that their toughness was as much façade as Oxford kids' respectability was. You could call it learned helplessness; it was certainly the more familiar form of phoniness. At least I knew what to do with it.

Even at the time I knew I wasn't happy, though happiness wasn't the goal. It was more about avoiding and resisting that crushing feeling of entrapment knowing someone else controls your fate. Most of my nights consisted of getting high at home or having some friends over to get high or finding some party to crash so we could drink and get high.

I definitely got mixed up in some things I shouldn't have, like the time I acquired a dao (Chinese saber) and broke into people's homes looking for whoever had been talking big about me, or the many times I smacked a white boy in the face for disrespecting me in public, or the time I rolled up to one white kid's doorstep with a bat looking to settle some longstanding beef. I earned beef with a lot of people back then, even people I'd never met, and that meant some kind of confrontation might go down at any time or place. Backing down was never an option, and if I ever got wind of a problem, I needed to dead the problem right away. It made me look decisive, but the truth was if I didn't my paranoia wouldn't let me sleep at night.

Death was all I thought about because dying felt like a very real possibility for me. This was after Columbine and the slow rise of gun violence in our schools, and then there was 9/11. Besides fearing gang-related or random violence, I received more than my share of racist aggression after these kinds of events. This was on top of the blatantly biased and often racist treatment of the police. On several occasions I would get busted along with some white kid, both of us for smarting off when police came to break up an underage party, and lo and behold the white kid would get a scolding and sent on his way, while Carlos had to be insulted or even brought down to the station just to waste his time.

It was a dark time, but I've always been one of those bull-headed types who would rather sabotage his own best interest than even appear to let someone push him around. So much of my life had been about proving everyone wrong—whatever they thought of me—rather than becoming a certain kind of person. I just couldn't take good advice, and I lacked the discipline to stick to any course for long. Instead, I held to a stubborn conviction that I'd always find a way to be all right—as long as "all right" was defined in the broadest sense.

It didn't take long for this lifestyle to take its toll on me. In quieter moments, alone in my room, I'd be wracked with guilt. *Did you really say that to that chick? Why did you mouth off to that guy? What are you doing with your life? Why are you so f*****g stupid?* In reality, the child that had hidden within me so long ago still lingered there, still desired a normal life. Inside, I liked people, enjoyed being around others, wanted to learn about different cultures, traditions, and lifestyles. I wanted to try new foods, hear new music, play party games. But I wanted to participate in all this life as an equal and not the weirdo from the streets, and that, it seemed, was an impossible request.

On the streets, this growing inner conflict expressed itself as having a hair-trigger for any perceived slight. At home, I turned to my life journal and tried to release my frustrations, doubts, and insecurities onto the blank page. One night early in this period, I came home feeling particularly inspired from having just seen Baz Luhrumann's *Romeo + Juliet*. I sat on my futon be with a pencil and my journal in hand, staring at the night sky, thinking about the person I had become and the story I had just watched and the man who, centuries ago, had written it. I picked up the pen and wrote to give the jumble in my mind some place to go, to let the feelings in my heart find some form:

> *Contemplation Life: Once upon a yesterday, one wished a sweet drop for bitter eyes. For to ask the request what for such misfortune in this existing life is simply to disregard one's own belief, which furthermore insults the world faith. Oh, what a web of indecisiveness have I constructed in my train of thought; yet, I must utter the word 'reason' for that is what I yearn.*
>
> *I feel as a mind out of place, as if the lion had been converted into the hyena with its mind still intact but out of place. A soldier is meant to endure hardships, wounds, and*

misfortune but what then of a soldier out of combat. What then is it to repetitively be in combat out of combat?

Times have come a distance as I have seen and fortune has placed me in "the land of the free," so they say. Many up spoken men have profited off her, America, and from them is where I obtain my reason, ambitions, and also maps. But yet, what good are the eyes in a nocturnal search when one has only but a box of matches to utilize.

I've an ongoing battle with good and evil with reason as a mediator. I've seen evil prosper with wickedness and aggression and with equivalence I've seen good prosper with humility and reverence. And yet, once again, I sit befuddled, unsure of what role I should play on this stage. Soon, but never the later, I shall conjugate both good, evil, and also reason and with perfect equilibrium impose each in everyday living including opposing circumstances.

I juggle extensively with life trying to comprehend one of many questions being purpose. As I commence to conjure a reply, I am halted by an intruding thought, begging to utter the question, "why do so." Since now and many years ago, I've fiddled with the question and only seemed to consume more questions. Therefore, a scientist will be riddled for days with an experiment. Till then one day he is overwhelmed with commonsense and knows where he faltered.

For to a complex mind is a good thing. But what of complexity when one is driven ever so gently towards the opposing road of sanity?

So henceforth, I shall alter my art of questioning and replace it with the simplicity of life. What simplicity this might be is in the eyes of the beholder. Now as I write, I am amused and astonished by my own contradictions of life.

There is only one person that can liberate me from troubles internally and externally. Whether you accept his existence or not, I for one do. Take this statement as desired; for if my goal were to give sweet melody to ears and ecstasy to eyes,

> *I would be a fool to myself and a false prophet to many. This one person, man, creator, spirit, or ruler is God, and to him, I'm thankful for the ability to write, think, act and speak in such a manner that astonished many. This here is but one of many more to come; my mind has a lot of seeds to plant, and this book is my garden.*

If all this sounds unsustainable, that's because it was, but it's also true that I was living a kind of Pareto principle of the hood where 80% of my problems came from where I spent about 20% of my time and energy. Most of the time, the switch was turned to the bright, warm Carlos who had potential. Both parts of me wanted to make something of myself, they just had different ideas of what that ought to look like.

Potential Carlos knew that I got into more trouble when I didn't have a job and that a job was one of the few places where I might be able to overcome my background by working within the system. I'd gotten my first paying job when I was fifteen. I would walk three miles to KFC three or four times each week, and it was a welcome respite from the chaos of home and the streets.

Work made sense to me. It was a structured environment with a simple purpose—not so unlike the streets. I'd watch the more experienced people and learn how to improve at each position they stationed me. I tried to learn every facet of every part of the business. I prided myself in being efficient, quick, and attentive to detail. Occasionally, I'd bend the franchise rules to make a task easier for me or just to give it a personal touch, and occasionally that would wind me up in hot water. The first time they put me up front as a cashier, genial Carlos lit up like someone had opened a fire hydrant. I got to gab with people and make them smile or laugh *as part of my job!* And here was something new: my managers appreciated how much work I got done. The equation was pretty simple: Hard work led to an appreciation of my value. That meant more, almost, than the paycheck.

Work let me be more myself under cover of fulfilling a set of responsibilities. I didn't have to be street Carlos or worry about what my brothers and sisters would think—or so I thought. The reality was that, at work or on the streets, it irked people to see someone succeed by being courteous, polite, well-mannered, and jovial. Envy is an ugly, destructive feeling, and I have been blessed with an ability to largely tune it out or, if anything, to believe that people should try to imitate me rather than want to bring me down. I've also learned that letting ugly emotions consume you is a surefire way to prevent your own success. The evidence of that was how many people had grown into old age without a substantial change in their situations. They were still living the same old street lives with the same old grudges and same old paralyzing attitudes. To this day, I have yet to meet a drug lord in the hood who started hustling as a kid and lived long enough to reach old age rich, powerful, and free.

My first job out of prison was as a dishwasher at a Ramada Inn. Then I worked as a dietary aide at a nursing home, a sales associate in a clothing store, a convenience store cashier, and a crater at a mattress spring factory. Working kept me out of trouble for part of the day, at least, and it introduced me to other working people in my community. In some cases, I knew my co-worker's kid, and the kid and I didn't necessarily care for one another, but I learned to like and respect the parent as we worked together. Other people came from different backgrounds or parts of the country, and I enjoyed learning about people without worrying about who was tougher. Later, I would appreciate the small network I had unwittingly built by simply making friends with people.

Work allowed me to move out of Mom's house and into an apartment I shared with this girl. It would soon become obvious that I did not thrive in an environment without any rules at all, which my roommate quickly grew to dislike, but in the meantime I met some people who would plant yet another seed of change in me. It turned out an old high school friend lived just across the street from my new place. He was a punk rocker whose aggressive appearance belied his nice and easy-going attitude, and he introduced me to his circle of misfits with screwed up pasts who, rather than fight amongst themselves, were warm and loving with one another. Whereas I had thought my past disqualified me from this kind of healthy, affirming community, these people showed me that our pasts had prepared us for just this kind of community. We had seen so much hurt that we understood better than most the importance of kindness. We had seen so much rejection that we understood the importance of acceptance.

But you know what I'm going to say: It didn't last.

I couldn't quite ditch my ghetto habits. Even when I had decent jobs, I would continue to hustle on the side for extra cash; I had dreams of buying a car and having more spending cash and generally being the adult I'd envisioned becoming. Some of my brothers thought hustling beat working for a meager paycheck any day. I'll say this for hustling: You could set your own hours, and any given score often felt like a bigger return than putting in two weeks of regular work. It wasn't regular work, though, and the costs of poor performance or even an honest mistake were much higher.

Around this time Mom started dating a guy with mafia ties; let's call him Lou. Lou was decent to me, treated me like an adult, and we grew to trust one another. I think he first started inviting me along on rides to get me out of the house and away from fights with Mom, but it turned into a positive for both of us. As he made drops at homes around town, we'd get to talking, and I impressed him with my analytic and strategic mind. He set himself up as a kind of mentor, and I in turn became something of a confidant.

Mafia drug running was a different ball game from the street hustle. We'd been part of a small crew of middle men mostly selling around our own neighborhoods. Lou was part of a whole distribution network that sold to middle- and upper-class households, many of whom would turn around and sell to their friends. It blew my mind to see him selling ounces of cocaine to the kind of guys you saw on television morning shows.

On the one hand, it took the whole concept of social respectability down yet another few notches for me; these were not the bland, corny, squeaky-clean people they presented themselves as. On the other hand, I was in awe of their ability to not only function but to live successful lives without drawing any suspicion upon themselves. As if I needed further proof of privilege.

Then one day, Lou told me about a deal he was brokering with some Colombians. They had wanted a little slice of mafia action in our territory, and Lou would represent his bosses at the meeting to negotiate the partnership. If things went well, there might be a role for me, but first he had to introduce me to his mob boss.

This was a man in his mid-forties who had somewhat recently taken over after the death of his father. Lou brought me to a storefront to meet him, and the first thing he said to me was, "You're Carlos, huh?" and shook my hand. Then he added, "Do me a favor, Carlos. Take those g**damn earrings off and let it be the last time you walk into my store with them on, okay?"

My gut twisted into a knot; he wasn't interested in hearing about my need to be myself.

"Yessir, sorry," I said as politely as possible.

He chuckled as he said, "Carlos, if you come in here like that again, I'll have to introduce you to my cousin Tommy. He's our retarded butcher who doesn't listen to anything I tell him to do."

I probably smiled back stupidly just because he was smiling, but I had no idea what he meant by that, and I only later understood he was trying to tell me there was no harm. In fact, by the end of that meeting I was in the clear and had been conscripted to help Lou build a network of buyers for the new Colombian partnership.

I tapped into my network and found several high-paying customers among them. Some were well-paid blue-collar guys who lived one life at home and another outside of it. Some of their wives and friends would join them for weekend ski trips, i.e., cocaine binges. I was like a regional sales manager earning decent money on commission.

We'd have to rub shoulders from time to time with the Colombians at the mafia version of a corporate event. The Colombians rubbed Lou and me the wrong way. To us, they seemed pompous and like they were playing at being down to earth. The Worcester mob's real interest in them was in their connections in New York, just like the Colombians' interest in us was in the Worcester area.

The Colombians also had more sophisticated transportation solutions. To protect their merchandise in transit, they set us up with a rigged Toyota Corolla, an inconspicuous vehicle with a hidden compartment. If you knew how to press the brake, turn the ignition, and fiddle with the hazards and high beams, a rectangular door popped open behind which might be six or seven kilos of cocaine. Guys in the hood would brag about handling a kilo when everyone knew they were lying; I got to handle more product in one night than my friends back in Lowell might see in a month.

Once the product made it to the pickup, we divided it evenly among ourselves. In order to make money at this game, you had to know how to cut the coke, that is, dilute it just enough that it goes farther while still being better than average for your market and still giving buyers room to cut it further for their own profit. Cutting involved acquiring a lot of specific ingredients from a vitamin or nutrition store, inositol (a supplement), acetone (a cleaning solvent), a spray bottle, C-clamps, 2"x4"s, respirator masks, latex gloves, vented safety goggles, heat lamps, shoe covers, garbage bags, newspaper, a toaster oven, and some special cleaning supplies for afterward.

Each producer had their own logo they'd use to distinguish their product—some used a photo of a person marked for death. They went to great lengths and used abundant layers of plastic, synthetics, petroleum jelly, and duct tape to protect the product. It was all highly scientific and smelled strongly no matter what precautions you took—imagine an unvented nail salon and multiply it by ten.

If only we had put that kind of energy and attention into something that didn't endanger people's lives (and our own), right?

The scale of the mafia operation started to make me nervous. It was one thing to put my own life on the line as a street hustler for the sake of being a high roller, scoring girls, and having a few brief thrills. It was another thing to get wrapped up in a world where getting on the wrong side of the wrong guy could have negative consequences for my sister. One doesn't just quit the mob, however. I was a "regional manager"; I was in too deep.

Thus I found myself once again living a double life, showing the mob the side of me that kept me safe and keeping the rest of me safe from their notice. I had dreamed of exceeding the other kingpins in the drug trade, but the small taste of success I'd had only made me miserable. I knew I had talent, and I looked around and saw so much incompetence among the guys higher up the chain than me, but I couldn't break through to the success I desired.

The mob runs an illegal business, but it's still a business. The same lack of discipline that made me a little too unpredictable for my legit managers also made me unreliable for more power on the black market. It would take many more years for me to appreciate what H. Jackson Brown, Jr., wrote in *Life's Little Instruction Book*:

> *Talent without discipline is like an octopus on roller skates. There's plenty of movement, but you never know if it's going to be forward, backward, or sideways.*

I was that octopus, but I didn't realize I had any real control over my disorientation. I had to ride the wave for a full year before my chance came to get out—and that was only because Lou cheated on Mom and they broke up. Getting fired for my boss's indiscretions was about the best-case scenario, though.

Meanwhile, I continued to pursue everything to excess. Many a Friday night of tripping on hallucinogens and dancing to entrancing beat of techno/house sounds led to a candy-flippin', rainbow-trippin', cowboy-crescent sniffin' cocaine off a girl's body weekend-long bender. I hopped from desperate housewives to bitter girlfriends to college singles, from career-driven mothers to rebellious daughters to vengeful sisters. Sometimes two at once. I would not slow down nor deny any lust or urge. In my head, I was a rock star.

In reality, I was out of control. As Newton's Third Law of Motion states, for every action there is an equal and opposite reaction. In the moral-emotional universe, those reactions could take months or years to manifest—but they always did. My depression deepened to the point that I resented the daylight for revealing the waste of space I had become. I'd gained everything I'd ever wanted and felt emptier than ever before. My motto was "All good things must come to an end," and a few months into my nineteenth year, it felt like the end was coming fast.

I looked in the mirror one day and didn't know who was looking back. The dreamer was still in there, trying to see some evidence of himself in the real world, but the man in the mirror was a waking nightmare. I was facing a lifetime of probation, had piles of court fees to pay, still, and no friends who shared my same secret desire to rise above all this. Something had to change, and I was the only one who could change it.

First thing on my agenda: Mellow out a bit. Ease off of Mom and try to roll with her mood swings. Next was to fill my down time, when boredom overcame me and turned into anxiety, with something more positive. For the first time ever, I voluntarily stepped foot inside a library and left with a stack of books in hand. I would teach myself the things I wanted to know, formal education be damned. I adopted a prison mindset, as if the only options available to me were to read or sleep, and I got down to studying.

I read history, psychology, poetry, and all sorts of things—including the Holy Bible. I studied WWII, 9/11, terrorism, the prison system, and stem cell research. Everything I learned sparked a dizzying burst of thoughts in my mind, so I journaled till my fingers ached. Then I watched or rewatched movies like *Romeo + Juliet*, *Scarface*, *Braveheart*, and the Godfather trilogy, paying close attention to how people treated each other, to the themes of sacrifice, trust, betrayal, and courage. Movies like *The Matrix*, *The Devil's Advocate*, and *Vanilla Sky* became like visual bibles to me as I unwound their layers of commentary about our moral reality and the significance of right and wrong, good versus evil, and the hero's redemption. It felt like reshaping my mind.

Mom and her boyfriend helped me find a place in Worcester where I could earn my GED. I went back to my old schoolbooks and finished reading them. I completed old homework assignments and worked on areas of weakness, especially math.

Still unaware of my ADHD or what it meant, I wrestled with frequent bouts of frustration. It felt like it took me three or four tries to read anything and understand it. Frustration would lead to anger, usually turned inward on myself for being, as everyone said, so bright but somehow unable to activate. I persevered, though, pushing harder and running faster to my goal. I needed to succeed to show God that I was done with my old life.

On November 5, 2003, I stood at a desk in a test center and took a printout that an admin handed to me. It said I'd passed the test and earned my GED. I'd cleared the hurdle, broke free of the past that had been haunting me. I began to imagine what it would be like to try on a new hat, jacket, and pants and present myself to the world as a new-made man.

THE GLASS HOUSE

All my life I have yearned for authenticity—in the way I lived my own life and in the way others dealt with me. Seems that's not too uncommon among us human beings. I had learned to define authenticity as expressing the darkest, unhappiest, and generally worst parts of myself, and as a consequence I had become a dark, unhappy, generally horrible person. It wasn't until I defined authenticity as living for my dreams that I began to like the person I was becoming. The GED was a big first step.

Next, I had to defeat my isolation. My defenses and self-hatred had been so strong that, at nineteen, I still didn't understand how intimate friendships worked. So, I sought out a new group of friends. I wound up with a crew that could have been writers for *Jackass*. The stupid and painful things they contrived when they got bored blew my mind, but I was happy to play along and join in the fun if that's what healthy friendships looked like.

I studied their tame white world. I learned to tone down some of my hood slang and to use words like *awesome* and *cool*. I loosened up when I met new people instead of assuming my serious, size-you-up hood stance. They accepted me into their group where they rarely fought and only insulted each other in a strange, new affectionate way. They taught me to laugh more, loosen up, not take everything so seriously or personally. In other words, my cred with them was established; I didn't need to be earning it every day.

We still did some of the same things I used to do with my friends from the hood, but we never did it in a way that went looking for or stirring up trouble. Rather than steal or destroy things, we had playful fun that was also generally pretty safe. And wouldn't you know that I was suddenly not getting into trouble with the law all the time?

Then it was time to get a new gig. A neighbor helpfully provided me a reference, and I quickly found a job at a convenience store nearby—a huge relief, as I didn't have a car. Now, I was at the center of the neighborhood's activity as good, hard-working people stopped in every morning for their coffee and paper and in the evening for their scratch tickets and beer. Tapping into my previous customer service experience, I addressed everyone with a "Yes, sir," and a "No, ma'am," and an "Enjoy the rest of your day!" Each new positive interaction helped me absorb the rhythm and pace of genuine neighborliness. I stopped focusing on what they had that I didn't and started to appreciate the ways we could connect.

In a funny way, I was learning to be average. How not to burst into a room and suck the air out of it with my need to be noticed while also not hiding in the corner like a mouse. How to accept people's casual greetings without needing to make sure they thought thus-and-so about me. If you'd told me a couple years back that I would become a cornball, a Carlton Banks, I'd have told you where to go, but now it was the thing I wanted more than anything. I was a tax-paying member of society with a GED. I had a good job where I was entrusted not only with handling the owner's money but with opening or closing the business. I had an apartment, a used 2003 Honda Accord, and a predictable routine.

Ironically, I took my normalcy back to my new friends' homes and became a good influence on them. Those nice white boys still got in trouble with drugs and alcohol, and their parents weren't at first too keen on them inviting over their baggy-pants-wearing Puerto Rican friend when they were already in hot water about an encounter with the cops. I was civil and polite, though, and earned their parents' trust. It got to where the parents would ask me to look after their kids when we went out partying. Most of the time we partied at my house, anyway, where I could control who was coming in.

For the first time in a long time, *I* meant more to *me* than anything or anyone else, and when things seemed their darkest, I never lost my drive to fight. I was creating a new Carlos, and as Mom had urged me as a three-year-old running beside her down three flights of stairs, I would never look back.

Becoming Boring

I couldn't tell you how I celebrated my 21st birthday—not because I was wasted, but because I wasn't. It was a boring, conventional day; I loved it. Four years earlier I'd turned 17 in lockup after living a more "exciting" life, and I didn't need any more of that nonsense. I'd approach 21 like the mature, responsible man I was becoming. No drama.

Enter Monica in my life. I met Monica at a house party, and she was the opposite of what a guy like me was supposed to be into. She was a tomboy, to begin with, who played school sports year-round. She always dressed in a T-shirt and basketball shorts, wore her hair in a ponytail, and never wore makeup. She earned straight A's, came from a modest, church-going home, and was on the shy side. She was perfect for the new, no-drama Carlos.

There was something unusual in her eyes that I didn't understand, at first. Later, I realized it was guilelessness and vulnerability, qualities I wasn't used to seeing in other people. Her eyes reflected back the hidden parts of my own soul, which I could never imagine revealing to someone again. That same innocence came through in her silly sense of humor and in the way, when we spoke, she listened as if she really cared about what I said. Meanwhile at home she had what I'd always longed for: happily married parents, a healthy relationship with her four siblings, a modest house in a decent neighborhood, a room where she could have peace and quiet. I wanted to be in her orbit and maybe soak up some of that stability.

I had screwed up love enough to not be in any great hurry to become deeply entangled with Monica right away. The old, pedal-to-the-floor Carlos had a knack for getting too deep in, getting scared, and screwing things up until both people were hurting. Or he'd realize he'd fallen for the wrong kind of girl only after she'd stepped all over him. I ruined my first true love when I got distracted by another pretty face and body. In the hood, that was just how us men were. But now I was changing my education level, my job status, my address, and my friends; it was time to change my love life.

Funny how, though I hadn't known much in the way of love growing up, I had always been looking for it. In my mind, love meant having a best friend to share a little slice of heaven with, full of laughter and warm smiles and no unnecessary sadness. A relationship with Monica promised just this, and I began to fall for her.

Initiate self-destruct sequence.

It took me only three months to screw things up with Monica. As long as I was keeping to my new life, I was a pretty good boyfriend to her. I treated her well, respected her, didn't constantly accuse her of sneaking around or any of the horrible stuff that was par for the course in my old life. The problem started when I went back to my old life for a last hurrah with my old group of friends in Oxford. We were partying on the beach on the Fourth of July, and I ran into my seventh-grade girlfriend. I was rolling on ecstasy and she was on mushrooms, and the minute our eyes locked we were like two animals. In our distorted mental states, it seemed like fate had thrown us together and we were only playing our parts. We reached for each other . . . and the rest was history, which is to say, history repeating itself.

When I returned home to my new normal, guilt overcame me every time I saw Monica. Not only did she trust me, but we'd started attending church together every Sunday morning. Faithfully. The moral conflict ate at my soul. I prayed silently to God for forgiveness, but a voice inside kept saying, *Confess to those whom you have sinned against.*

If confessing my guilt was my only way out of Hell, I would have hanged myself trying to escape. Each time I looked in her eyes, the memory of that illicit night returned to me and convicted me of how badly I'd treated her. Each time I sat beside her in the pew, I felt the pastor speaking directly to me, alone. *I'm a good person, I know I am,* I'd pray to myself. *What I did was wrong—a regrettable mistake, weakness I fell into once again—but You, Lord, know my heart and how much pain I harbor for what I did. I simply ask that you heal my soul so I can get on with it already.*

What hurt the most was she'd chosen me—a filthy, good for nothing, sex-obsessed loser—to lose her virginity to. Back in the hood, the girls mostly learned to keep their expectations pretty low. It wasn't fair to them, of course, but at least it was an open secret that we guys could show them a good time but were unreliable for most everything else. Monica had grown up with normal, or at least healthy expectations of what a guy should be like, and I'd fallen way short.

To compensate, I overcompensated. I demeaned myself as a scumbag, a sinner, an unfixable bum. I elevated her as an angel, pure as the driven snow. I put myself through hell and tried to make her life heaven. For months this went on. I thought my suffering would eventually purge my sin, so I endured it quietly.

The straw that broke the camel's back came when we saw the film *The Passion of the Christ*. It so vividly represented the physical suffering of Jesus Christ, who'd done nothing wrong, and who endured it all for sinners like me. I felt vain for thinking my private suffering for my sin was somehow heroic or brave; I had to tell Monica.

"There's something extremely important I need to tell you," I said on the drive home that night. She smiled uncertainly back at me. Back at the house, I slowly told the story, factually and without attempts at justifying myself. By the end she was crying like a child who'd been forcibly pulled away from her mother. Seeing her fall apart like that destroyed me, too. I felt the full weight of my disgrace; I felt insignificant, a big nothing compared to the grandeur of her presence.

Even this was a turning point for me. I had never hurt anyone so totally before, nor had I ever confessed so honestly. Had we had an explosive fight, I would have said more hurtful things and stormed off, then we would have ended it and I would have carried on unchanged. Because she instead simply revealed to me her hurt, and because I was remorseful enough not to take advantage of it, I was able to genuinely unburden myself. With that confession came years of pain, hurt, and dark things I had been holding in. Telling this one truth scraped clean years of secrets and lies. It didn't fix the problems I'd created with them, but it released me from their power. It was a small moment of grace in a life full of guilt and shame.

Monica proved stronger than I even knew. She didn't immediately drop me, but with a lot of work, some help from her mom, and a lot of time, she eventually forgave me. We cleared the mess away and began rebuilding what looked like a bright future together. I started going to church twice a week, forfeited my old friends and habits. I went from indulging every desire to avoiding every form of sin I could. I took refuge in the routine; the routine kept Monica and me together.

It was a sunny morning in April 2004. I wore a light blue dress shirt with a grey tie, black slacks and black pleather shoes I bought at *Payless*, and I walked into the collections agency offices like I already had the job. I had been doing some work through a temp agency, which I used as a kind of loophole for a guy with a criminal record to get in the door. I hoped to demonstrate my value such that it would overshadow my past. It worked.

"How's it going? I'm Jack Tammano, and you are . . ." said a gruff, middle-aged man who was walking through the front office. For whatever reason he had stopped to talk.

"Carlos Ricard. Nice to meet you," I said and shook his hand.

"You can call me Jack. Who are you waiting for?"

"Mack. I'm here for the telemarketing position."

"Mack's running a bit late, but come into my office while you wait for him."

"Okay, sir—I mean, Jack." I followed him into his office and took the seat he indicated. He walked around his desk and got comfortable in his own chair.

"Where you from, Carlos?"

"Oxford. About an hour from here."

"If you don't mind my asking, do you speak Spanish at all?"

"Yes, I do. I read and write it," I said, then added with a smirk, "but I speak English more better."

That quip got me a job by the man who would become my first real mentor in business—legitimate business, that is. He was also the president of the company: Jack, the Wolf of Debt Street. He was an unstoppable force, a freak of nature; a short, Italian American *Masshole* who could talk a snake into giving up its skin.

I'd never met anyone like him. He took a real passionate interest in teaching and molding others into better versions of themselves. It turned out that was partly by necessity;

most people did not walk through the doors with the thick skin and confrontation skills necessary for collections, so he had to make them into what he needed. He had zero tolerance for half-truths, bull****t, or pity parties. He didn't want to hear excuses and he didn't care how hard your life was. We thought he could read minds; he could catch the slightest inconsistency or inflection and call out a lie. He wasn't afraid to get in your face if he had to straighten you out. After all, he had a business to run.

Jack's talent for collections fascinated the intellectual in me, which I think made me an ideal student. He initiated me into the dog-eat-dog world of collections where all the usual social conventions and civilities no longer applied—unless they were useful, that is. My job, in effect, was to confront people with their mistakes and ask them how they planned to fix things. That is to say, my job was to start fights with people all day—how happy would you be to get a call like that? It was collectors versus debtors. We were the hunters, and the prey was slippery and deceitful.

It turned out growing up in an environment where you had to stay constantly vigilant lest things suddenly turn ugly and violent gave me some advantages as a collector. I understood making mistakes, and I understood making excuses for why you shouldn't be held responsible, but I also understood that collections was the end of the road; there was only one relevant question, now—How are you going to pay? Compassion is good and all, but it doesn't change the truth of someone's actions.

For each of my first twelve months, I beat my prior month's collections. My commissions kept going up and I suddenly found myself with more money. I upgraded from a '91 Pontiac 6000LE to the '03 Accord and found a beautiful studio apartment in an old converted art-deco luxury hotel. I felt like I had found the secret key to unlocking real upward mobility.

Upward mobility and financial stability came at a cost, though. While I excelled at work, the endless pressure to outdo myself each month started to stress me out. The danger of losing my job certainly motivated me, but I wouldn't say it inspired me or helped work feel in any way fulfilling. The commute took an hour each way, and I had to constantly ask for leniency in arriving late or leaving early to make court dates. Add to that the way Jack rode me constantly. He saw potential in me, and his way of building me up involved a lot of tearing down along the way. You don't become a dopehead if you're good at managing stress, and now I had this white guy putting me on the spot in meetings, dissecting my every word and action, and telling me he needed to mold my brain "because it's full of mush." I thought constantly about quitting, but where else would a guy with my record go?

Jack was, indeed, molding me, irksome as it could be. He berated and corrected and shoved me along the path to becoming the cutthroat businessman I needed to become to survive in the industry. I'd always been a resilient kid; I had to be to survive. I didn't realize how sensitive the hood could make you, though. There, getting in someone's face usually led to violence. We lived and died by a code of respect in public that masked disdain behind closed doors. Words were as harmful as sticks and stones, and everyone was a potential enemy.

Jack set about unprogramming what I'd learned in the hood. I had to learn to deflect words in the name of a greater goal than my own honor. I had to learn that not everyone responded to respect with respect, and it wasn't a reflection on me. I had to learn that image could only take you so far, that I needed to invest in my own personal growth and success. I had to learn how to detect the sometimes subtle deceptions and half-truths people told sometimes without even knowing they were doing it.

I had thought leading a strait-laced life would help me bring the inner and outer Carlos together. Ironically, however, I replaced one double life with another. Instead of acting the tough guy on the streets all day, I was the cold-as-ice collections agent. Instead of the curious, warm kid who studied the stars in his room, I was the upright churchgoer praying to my heavenly Father. Worshipping at our church allowed me to unload the burdens of darkness and sin I had gathered over the week and to refuel my soul with hope and love. By Wednesday, I'd feel emptied out again.

As I always had, I was flying by the seat of my pants, without a compass, a map, or a trusted guide. I couldn't even tell if I was going off course, but I knew something was wrong. I had built a house of glass—pretty to look at, but impossible to live in.

Monica went off to college. She turned 21. I wanted to trust her, but I had no context for believing an inexperienced white girl could avoid the temptation of partying and all the irresponsible behaviors that came with it. Moreover, I was too familiar with the party lifestyle. I told her it would be fine as long as she remained up front with me and was careful about her friends, but I couldn't control my obsessive thoughts.

As college opened up her world and she made interesting new friends, she began to change. She'd forget to call me and say she fell asleep studying. She'd come over less because she had homework and things with her friends. They were understandable changes, but they triggered thoughts and ideas from my old life that I couldn't shake off. I grew convinced she was lying to me, and if there's one thing a guy from the hood cannot tolerate it's his woman lying to him.

Looking back, my confession had been the beginning of the end for us. While I had made myself legitimately vulnerable to her in that moment, I hadn't taken as much responsibility as I should have. I told the story in such a way that my friends appeared at least partially responsible for letting me get so high and not stopping me. I didn't even need to blame them directly; Monica did it for me. It helped the pill go down. And though we worked through some of the surface difficulties, we were too immature to appreciate how deep and raw the wound was. I had held just enough back that we couldn't really say we'd dealt with the whole issue.

Now that she was becoming an independent adult, I think we both started to realize how difficult it was to bridge the gap between our backgrounds. I'd fallen in love with her when she was innocent and I had committed more than my share of sins. I wanted her to be my rock, my reason for staying on the right path. I thought God brought us together so we would marry and grow old together. She was the one I could be the new me with. But she still had some years of maturing to do, some mistakes to make. Somehow, I was the old bore in the relationship, the possessive one who didn't want her to have any fun. Of course, I was worried about her, knowing what kind of trouble someone can get into at a party, but I didn't exactly begrudge her hanging out with her friends and drinking and what not. It was more that I couldn't handle her changing, and she hadn't really healed from the pain of my transgression.

I had been living a fantasy of love cobbled together from TV and Hollywood movies, a needy, one-sided kind of love that took and took and panicked when the source was removed. It was a love that always kept a piece of me in reserve behind defense mechanisms. The minute I felt I'd lost control of the situation, I panicked, and anger took over. I was no longer Carlos—I became my mother. And I would say some of the nastiest, cruelest things to protect myself. I'd feel like crap afterwards, but instead of trying to fix things, I'd pull another trick from Mom's playbook and simply act as if nothing had happened. I was completely blind to the lasting effects of the pain I'd caused—so much so that I'd get angry when old wrongs were dug up and thrown back at me. At the same time, some part of me deep down knew I'd royally messed up.

Ghetto me would have fallen apart in a self-destructive binge of sex and drugs under these circumstances. Respectable me decided to dig deeper into work. It was where I spent the most time outside of the time I spent obsessing about Monica. I'd spent five or six days a week with these people for every week of the last three years, after all. If they weren't my people, who were?

At this point I'd become a supervisor and was earning more money than I'd ever seen, even in my mafia days. I'd achieved a mediocre success and a bland routine. My work friends were all right and mostly kept me out of trouble, but the fact was that I was associating myself with master manipulators, professional prevaricators, and distinguished deceivers; I couldn't help but become more like them. The world of collections repeated the same logic of self-preservation in an unfair world that I'd learned on the streets, only the methods were different—and legal.

They were all mostly white, with typical white backgrounds; I felt like I was from another planet. It was little things, like which TV shows and movies we loved, what music we listened to. I was into boxing; they were into football. There were bigger things, too, like how easily I'd react with biting anger. It was the ghetto in me that assumed anger was always justified, and I thought it was how Jack had taught me to act. I had no self-awareness that others found it overly harsh. When I led the pack in my collections, I'd be riding high and intolerably vain; when I was low, I was unapproachable.

Jack wouldn't tolerate any mouthing off to him; he always made sure I knew who the alpha male was. In addition to straight up getting in your face and telling you what you did wrong, he had psychological tactics. He would work you until he could get into your mind and use what he found there to get more productivity out of you. He'd find out about our personal lives and hang them over our heads, like, "What are you gonna tell your wife if you can't get your numbers up and I have to fire your ass?" or, "C'mon, you don't want to have to move back in with your mommy, do you?" He saw me as a hard nut to crack, like trying to jack the Batmobile. It irked me, but as I learned to protect myself from his manipulations I grew stronger, and he grew to trust me more. He took me on golf outings, gave me a VIP ticket to a Bruins game, introduced me to Scotch and cigars, and brought me around to meetings and parties with successful business people in the city.

I played along, but I couldn't help feeling like a phony who would soon be discovered and kicked out. Moreover, I wasn't happy with the man I'd become at work, but I also wasn't happy with the man I'd become at home. I tried to ignore the drugged-up street thug living inside me, but he gnawed at me, objecting to how normal and safe my life had become. To keep him quiet, I began to secretly give him small doses of what he wanted behind everyone's backs. A couple of hits of a joint here, a few beers there, maybe a shot or two and I was good. It allowed me to convince myself that I was more self-disciplined and put-together than I was. Everything I'd built felt so much more fragile and delicate than I'd expected it to be. I didn't know how much longer I could keep it all up.

Then a stranger called me on the phone. "You're mother's in the hospital," she said.

Making Peace with Mom

My mother had moved to Orlando with a guy she'd met about six months after breaking things off with Lou. She had decided she'd had enough of New England winters, and this guy had family down there who could help get them set up. This was in the spring of 2005; Laura was twelve and starting to look more like a young woman than a little girl. Laura and I had always had a very open relationship because I felt it was important she had someone in her life she could talk to about anything. As we said goodbye outside of the U-Haul the day they left, I made sure she knew that didn't change just because she'd be 1200 miles away.

That was about a year ago. "She was in the emergency room, and then she stopped breathing and collapsed to the floor," Mom's friend had told me. That raised some questions, obviously, but there was more to the story. Once in the ER, Mom suddenly lost the ability to breathe on her own and collapsed. Doctors couldn't get a breathing tube past her gag reflex, and instead of a tracheotomy they induced a coma and then hooked her up to the breathing machine. Tests showed her lungs were full of water, meaning she was drowning from the inside, but they couldn't determine why. They made an incision in her lungs to empty out the water, but they would have to pump her full of steroids to keep things in check. Problem was, they had to inject the steroids directly into her heart rather than use the IV, and for that they needed legal permission. As her oldest child, I was the nearest legal proxy. That was what the call was about.

All I understood was that this was the best way they knew to keep her alive, so I consented over the phone. They said they had some paperwork, too, that I would need to sign in order to continue with the treatments. Later that day I boarded a plane to Orlando, having bought a ticket with my rent money. Suddenly I understood why Jack always bugged me to, "put some money aside for an emergency".

The flight gave me almost six hours to think about my relationship with my mom. The thought of losing her scared me, not only because of the love a son can't but feel for his mother but because I didn't know what I would do with all the anger and grief I'd stored up against her. I nursed a grudge for every horrible thing she had done to me; I carried my past of abuse around like an anchor tied to my waste.

 I didn't deserve the things she did to me, but I knew she also didn't deserve a lot of the stuff I did to her. I dished it right back to her, sometimes, and I made it tough for her to juggle work and parenting and relationships. Deep down, I knew that simply blaming her for everything was not only unfair but would actually hurt me, too, rotting my potential from the inside out. By the time I walked into her hospital room and saw her unconscious on the bed, the only thing I wanted was to hear her voice again.

 Nothing compares to the psychological fuckery of trying to wrap your head around the idea that your mother, who is lying nearly lifeless in front of you, may never wake up again. Your hands will never feel a sadder touch than the hands of someone who may never hold you back. Your eyes will never witness a more painful scene than the sleep that no amount of money, science, status, or desire might break. Your lips will never utter more tragic words than those you should have spoken before it was too late.

 A nurse explained to me that they rarely saw this condition in people my mother's age. More to the point, they still weren't sure what caused it and thus how to fix it. For now, the machine was doing 80% of Mom's breathing.

 "If there's any information you can find out and share with us, it'll help us figure out the best way to treat her," she said. I latched onto that as a mission, a concrete task I could direct my energy toward. I dug through my memory bank for any information Mom might have told me. I thought about our family's medical history—what I knew of it—and about the various self-destructive behaviors Mom had gotten up to.

 Then it dawned on me: Their new apartment had lots of black mold growing under the kitchen sink, in the bathroom, and in other places around the house. They'd been complaining to the landlord for months, and he kept promising to do something but never acting. It was so bad, Laura started getting paralyzing headaches.

Mom's friend later told me that Mom, Laura, and the new boyfriend had finally decided to move and were packing just days before. That eventually led to Mom being in the ER in the first place. She and her boyfriend had gotten into an ugly argument while packing. I'm sure Mom said some hurtful, awful things, but this guy sounded like a piece of work, too. Things took a violent turn when he went to the shed and came back with a wrench. Right there in front of Laura, he takes a swipe at her head. She only partially blocked it and recoiled, screaming from the pain and in utter disbelief. He threatened to kill her and tried to restrain her, but she fought herself free and ran for the door.

Poor Laura grabbed a knife and warned him to leave Mom alone, but he was seeing red. He caught Mom, punched her, then hits her in the head with the wrench again. Mom fought him back enough to finally escape out the front door, and Laura, momentarily frozen in fear, snapped out of it and escaped out the back.

Mom ran into the middle of the street screaming for help from the neighbors. The boyfriend took a step out the door, but as people had started to notice something going on, he got cold feet and retreated back inside. Mom's friend hurried over and drove her to the ER, after which she collapsed.

It got scarier. From the looks of things, this wasn't just about a domestic spat getting out of control; this sick S.O.B. had been planning something for some time. That day, he had hidden her cell phone, and he had placed the wrench on a high ledge where only he could reach it. The cops inspected the shed thoroughly and also found rope and duct tape stashed inside a black garbage bag in the back. It's possible he had dreamt up something even more perverse than what he wound up doing.

He was arrested and given a hefty bail he wouldn't ever post, and that was the last we ever heard from him.

Of course, no amount of justice could change Mom's condition. The breathing machine pumped air in and out of her lungs with an eerie, shushing rhythm. *Fshhh... Frrrrh... Fshhh... Frrrh...* The EKG beeped out her heartrate in counterpoint. *Fshhh-beep-beep-Frrrh-beep-beep.* The sounds entranced me as I sat staring at her, clouding away the rest of the world. It was time for me to deal with Mom, once and for all.

As much hurt and unresolved pain as there was between us, she was still the strongest woman I knew. *God, this can't be it for her,* I prayed. *This can't be how it ends.* I wanted to show her love, something we'd been uncomfortable doing in the past. I held her hand and rubbed her fingers and started talking to her, recalling as many good memories as I could. I remembered the laughs, the hugs and kisses, all the gifts and toys. The time she and Ralph got married and I cried, thinking they were going to abandon me, only to learn that they were in fact making a new home for me. I couldn't help but also think of some of her mistakes—and many of mine, too—but of how she'd always had my back after all was said and done.

Then I recalled the song she used to sing to me as a child: "Mama, yo soy Carliiiitooo. ¡No hago travesuuura!" *Mama, I am Carlito. I don't make any trouble.* I couldn't fight it any longer and broke down weeping.

Suddenly, her hand gripped mine, then loosened. I couldn't tell if she had done it intentionally, but if there was any chance she could hear me, I had to take it. I needed her and God to hear me out.

I began with a sincere apology for the way I had treated her over the years. I forgave her for the way she had treated me, something that took an event of this significance for me to find the power to do. I assured her that I would look after

Laura, she didn't need to worry about that. I caught her up on my life, on work and church and Monica. Then I began to pray over her, talking to our Father in Heaven. I knew God had sustained us through everything, and I believed He would pull her out of this coma.

For a long time, I just let everything out, spoke whatever I felt moved to speak. It seemed like I had arrived in a place with her where I had always wanted to be. Only now, when she was at her most fragile, could we get there. Again I felt the peeling away of layers of pain and the lifting of a great weight. It was very likely a one-sided experience, but I took anything I could get.

At the mention of Laura's name, her hand had tightened again. It seemed she was in a secret fight with death, and I spoke words of encouragement and hope over her to empower her to fight harder. Before I left for the room they'd prepared for me down the hall, I kissed her on the cheek and told her, "You're not done living yet, Mom. You have fought too hard to give up now. You have too much left to witness Laura and me achieve. Come back to us."

For several days I lived with the very real possibility that I would become the primary caretaker of a 13-year-old girl. Ralph would be no help. I called him to tell him what was going on, including what it might mean for his daughter, but he shrugged it off as interesting news that didn't concern him.

Meanwhile, I roamed around the streets of Orlando trying to keep my head clear. To my surprise, I saw all around me a thriving Latino culture. Latinos walked around the streets proudly. Latinos owned not only restaurants, body shops, and clothing stores but insurance companies and auto dealerships. Latinos ran not one but several radio stations. Black, brown, and white lived together without pretending to all be like each other. For the first time in my life I felt like I fit in rather than stood out. I didn't feel like I had to choose between being a street-bred Rican or a preppy white kid. I didn't feel that constant suspicion that anyone outside the hood or the gang or the city or what-have-you was somehow out to get you. I didn't feel that implicit belief that success was not for us or that self-destructive urge to tear down anyone who started to make something of themselves. I felt like I could just be me, and it moved me deeply. Something was changing in me.

Fortunately, Mom kept improving until, finally, they announced they could move her to a new room and wake her up. It was around noon on a Thursday that they told us Mom was up and we could go see her. When we entered the room, Mom was clearly confused. She'd had no concept of what had happened and was surprised to see me down in Florida. Laura broke down into tears. I told her the gist, told her I lover her, and asked her to promise never to smoke again, to take better care of herself for my and Laura's sake. Mom got emotional, too, tearing up and admitting she had missed me. She agreed to take better care of herself and thanked me for being a good son to her when she most needed me.

I left for home later that day; I had to get back to work.

On the flight home, I felt again the press of the question, "Who is Carlos J. Ricard?" Orlando had helped me imagine a different way of interacting with and presenting myself to the world that didn't make me choose among the different sides of my identity. That made it difficult to just fall back into the old patterns.

Within six months of Mom's close call, my abuelo, Encarnacion, suffered a massive stroke. This was it; he was on his way to the Big Man above. I had some money for a change, so I bought Mom a ticket, too, and soon we were heading to Puerto Rico to see him off.

My abuelo was about the hardest-working person I knew. He farmed 16 acres on a steep hill which he would climb several times a day. Long ago he had been an abusive alcoholic, but my abuela gave him an ultimatum: clean up or get lost. He became a devout Catholic who never missed Mass and prayed for us all three times a day. Now in his 90s, the stroke had brought him low. He could no longer see, could hear very little, and one side of his body was paralyzed. It had struck at night, and he'd fallen on the floor and lain there for hours until Abuela woke up.

Though he couldn't see us, he recognized me by my voice immediately. Neither Mom nor I could bear to see him so frail, hardly able to raise his hand to greet us. It was an emotional time for the whole gathered family. At different times we might be laughing, crying, smiling contentedly, or frowning heavily. We shared stories upon stories, remembering his love of us. His presence, story, journey, and his last days left an everlasting mark on me. He showed me what a man looked like, what dedication really meant, and how sincerely and deeply a man could change—and how that could alter the lives of his 14 living children.

It also felt great to be back among my warm, supportive extended family. Here were people who told me I had something special in me when I confided that I wanted to do something big in my life. Their embrace of me brought me back to my roots of who I had always been because they saw that person still inside me, whatever else I had become.

TRYING TO TAKE ROOT IN BAD SOIL

The resurrection plant survives by blowing where the wind takes it until it can put down roots and grow. It only takes a little moisture to begin the process, but that little moisture may not be enough. Just like a late frost can kill an early blooming flower, that moisture can disappear and leave the resurrection plant exposed to the elements it had been protecting itself from.

I had been trying to blossom, but if living respectably to prove to everyone I wasn't some ghetto Rican was like seeking nourishment from a bad source, then what happened next was like trying to take root in bad soil. Of all the lessons I could have learned from Orlando and Puerto Rico, the one I told myself was that I needed to stop keeping the impulsive, self-destructive, "true" Carlos in check. That I should set him free to do whatever he pleased. It wasn't like I had any models or even wise advisors to help me, here. I only had my background and upbringing and experiences of the world to work with.

This would lead me down a familiar dark path which, looking back, may have been to some extent necessary for me to finally purge my psyche of both the demons of my faulty street logic and the false angels of my notions of success, to bring the inside and outside of me together into something like a real life. I started hanging out with the old crowd, took up weed behind Monica's back, and let mild buzzes turn into hangovers. Small arguments with Monica escalated into huge fights, which led to us spending less time together and to me doing more things behind her back. I could no longer tolerate the double standard by which she accepted other people's wild behaviors but couldn't stand mine. Though I had created the problem, I decided I was done being punished for it. Though she was only trying to protect herself, I think she came to represent to me all the forces trying to keep the "true" Carlos buried under the surface.

Monica was still safe, somehow, though we held our relationship together with a thin string. Whenever things picked up a little, I would buy her all sorts of gifts. When things were down, I'd blow money on whatever just to have something to do. I was bad at managing money and staying on top of bills at the best of times, but now that I was trying to buy more time with Monica, I was getting into some serious trouble. If I wasn't careful, I was going to be on the receiving end of a call from . . . well, someone like me. There were cracks all through my glass house. I was trying to put roots down into dry sand. It's possible that deep down I was trying to blow it all up, that I couldn't see my way out, so I found an excuse to tear it all down.

While the pressure built up around me, pride and comparison prevented me from being really honest with myself. Pride convinced me I was justified in any and all actions and in any offense I took for how people responded to them. Comparison caused me to believe I wasn't as bad as the people I had surrounded myself with. Pride was wrong, of course, in that no one is justified in hurting others or spending money they don't have. Comparison was wrong, too. I wasn't like my friends because I had massive debt and lived under strict probationary guidelines and I had no real social supports to fall back on when my life fell apart—or was blown up—around me. What's more, I had a long history of bad decision making and a laundry list of failures to show for it.

My anxiety and depression ramped up with a vengeance, and as winter of 2008 was slowly fading into spring, I finally lit the fuse on the bomb I'd been building in my life and through away four years of progress. It would take another year, but eventually I would shatter my glass house and run headfirst into the welcoming arms of county prison.

I felt like the subject of the Sinatra lyric, "You're nobody till somebody loves you." Somebody finally loved me, and I finally felt like somebody. It never dawned on me that defining myself in that way made me vulnerable should we ever break up, and we were headed toward breaking up. For some reason, I convinced myself that it would be a stage, a temporary separation that would allow us to get some of the negative junk out of our systems, help her see what a good thing we had. A break-up would show her a real-world lesson better than any lectures I could give her. Then we would reunite and be stronger and closer than ever.

Obviously, I wasn't thinking as clearly as I should have been.

One night, we argued again, but this time it sent me over the edge. I took off and spent the night at a bar throwing back Scotches like I was in the Rat Pack. Monica found me after I'd come home and passed out in bed. She woke me up crying and screaming like I'd murdered someone. Feeling not only justified but now falsely accused of all manner of things, I spat back at her, "You're lucky I don't have two bi****s in this bed right now!"

But she wasn't lucky, and I wasn't such a baller that I could follow through on a threat like that. Something in my mind told me I was, though, and that it was a sure means of hurting her and thereby protecting my flimsy ego.

The next day I answered a knock at the door to find Monica, a friend of hers, her friend's boyfriend, and a state trooper. They came in and began collecting Monica's things, including her big-screen television. The trooper assured me he was only there to make sure "things went smoothly." Though I knew this was coming, I still felt blindsided. I reacted by laughing at the "absurd theatrics" of Monica walking stone-faced back and forth in front of me as if I were invisible. After they left, though, I fell back on the couch, still dumbfounded and trying to process it all through the fog of my hangover.

Monica thought I had become a certain kind of man, but she had no idea what I was capable of, and that day she gave me all the permission I needed to show her and anyone else who needed to know. I felt betrayed, trampled on, discarded like a gum wrapper—which meant I felt angry. If there was one thing no human being was going to make me feel again, it was like trash. I wouldn't let anybody slap their ignorant and unjust labels on me; I would give them good reason to know they were right. You think I'm some abusive, possessive, macho, psycho boyfriend? All right, I can do that.

While I felt like I was at my breaking point, the total devastation of my life didn't happen all at once. Monica and I talked and even started seeing one another again for a little while, though we broke it off again a few weeks later. The problem was that we didn't trust one another. She would tell me crazy stories about her job tending bar near school and then lie to me about not getting into anything herself (at least, I was pretty sure they were lies). Meanwhile, I told myself that if anybody was going to be partying it up, it was going to be me; it was practically a second career for me. When I found out she had gotten a tattoo, I went out and got my own—the Puerto Rican coat of arms, a symbol of pride hands I told him I wanted out in my family and heritage. I went back to Lowell and started making connections with people who made me feel important even if getting too close to them could wind me up in jail. In fact, I spent a night in jail after an incident where I freaked out and refused to pull over for some cops because I'd had two beers that night. I started living it up like I was in my teens again. I drank and smoked and brought a bunch of girls home, but all I could think about was Monica.

Reconnecting with guys in the hood showed me both what happened to the life I left and how similar people are anywhere you go. My boy Ricky, with whom I could always pick right up no matter how long it had been, told me the news and how Felo and Booma had each served time for different things and how Snake Eyes was never heard from again. King Fear, to my utter and total shock, turned out to be an undercover informant for the FBI. When that came out, he fled the state and was also never seen again. So much for "no snitching." Whether in the hood or in the office, it seemed like everyone who made it was either cutthroat or crooked, bent the rules to suit themselves, or simply inherited their wealth. The rest of us who tried to follow "the rules" often got screwed.

I still believed Monica and I would eventually reunite as a couple, but I decided to take a friend's advice and get back out there, this time armed with a new MySpace page. I created my account and filled out my profile and all, then almost immediately looked up Monica. The first thing I saw, of course, was her profile picture. In it, she was in a very Goth Halloween costume, her mouth wide open and her tongue sticking way out. Opposite her was some Goth guy with his tongue out, too—touching hers.

This may not seem like such a big deal, but my reaction was visceral, reflexive, out of my control. My mind raced. My anxiety went haywire. My nerves vibrated so much that my hands trembled like a Parkinson's patient's. My heart pumped blood through my veins like a captain ordering his crew to save a sinking ship. This was the girl who had always been too shy to kiss me in public. This was my image of innocence, my model of modesty, and my paragon of purity. I'd told myself she was too naïve and sheltered to really act out in the ways I feared, but here was evidence that I was wrong. Way wrong. What else did I not know?

I took a break but could not get myself back together enough to work, so I told Jack what happened and he, knowing how easily I could ruin years of hard work, gave me the rest of the day off. The last thing I wanted was to be alone, so I hit up a long-time friend and told him that all I wanted to do was to drink as much as was humanly possible. We bought some Bacardi from a liquor store and did just that until the wee hours of the night.

He begged me not to drive home, but I'd have had to believed I was responsible for my actions to take that advice seriously. The whole twenty-minute trip, I drunk-dialed Monica, but she wouldn't pick up. I knew she was ignoring me, so I stopped at a payphone and tried again. She picked up.

"Hello, who's this?" she answered.

"You dirty, f*****g wh***," I slurred.

"Who the hell is this?"

"You know who this is, you dirty, f*****g wh***! I saw your profile picture on MySpace, you dirty piece of s*** wh***! You lied to me, you f*****g b****!"

"What are you talking about? What picture?" she asked, genuinely confused.

"Don't act like you don't know! I'm not going to be your stupid f*****g fool, anymore."

"Ha-ha," she laughed. "Oh please, that? That means nothing. Are you calling me drunk?"

"You tongue-slamming another guy and posting the picture is *nothing* to you now, huh, you dirty f*****g wh***?"

The line went dead. I swore to myself for a few seconds, then called her back.

"What, you wanna insult me some more?" she answered.

"Why did you lie to me? *Why?*"

"Lie to you about what?"

"Stop acting like the dumb, innocent b**** I thought you were."

The line went dead again, and I was left there with the receiver in my hand and the knowledge that I'd said to her some of the cruelest things I'd ever said to a woman before or since.

Street Carlos was in the ascension, so the street patterns took over. I cursed the ground she walked on and damned the day for shining on her and the night for giving her rest. I couldn't work enough, exercise enough, or ingest enough drugs or booze to alleviate the pain and sadness inside. I would torture myself—if there was one thing I was good at, it was torturing myself to death—by remembering the good times that were long gone and then imagining what partying and screwing she might be up to while I was crying in my room, alone, high, and wishing I had her back. I blamed myself for not having the mental stability to keep a girlfriend. I blamed God for making me believe my life could be normal and for letting me fall so hard for someone so duplicitous and even believe it was His plan for us to marry, then I prayed desperately for Him to save me from it all.

Somewhere in that timeless time, I reconnected with my cousin Sheila. Mom had been arrested for a DUI and called Sheila, and Sheila had called me to tell me about it, and we started talking on the phone once in a while. Sheila lent me a kind ear and gave me advice I wouldn't be able to hear until I hit rock bottom again. She told me it was up to me, as the oldest of my family, to change the course and direction of my family tree. If I didn't do it, the cycle could just continue in my kids and my sister and my sister's kids.

Sheila and some other family I had reconnected with following Abuelo's passing gave me homes to spend the holidays with. For four years, I had relied upon Monica's family to replace the family I didn't have. Now, I showed up at aunts' and uncles' and cousins' homes like a lost puppy begging for scraps. Thankfully, they welcomed me as they always did and kept me safe for a little longer.

The Barbaric Sport of Gentlemen

My depression and aimlessness eventually brought me to a bar up the road from me called the *Galloway Bay*, an Irish pub a Puerto Rican kid like me wouldn't normally be caught dead in. I ordered a beer and looked up at the TV screens, where I saw this crazy-ass white-person game of men running and slamming into each other without pads or helmets. The bartender, a young guy named Grant, gave me a rundown of this barbaric sport played by gentleman and known by the name of rugby. He said the local team was holding tryouts soon and invited me to give it a go.

I hadn't played sports since Little League, but I was young and fit and full of aggression looking for an outlet, so I figured, *Why not?* Soon I was a B-Side member of the Worcester Rugby Football Club.

Rugby is a European sport mostly played by beastly looking white guys from the British Isles, Australia, and New Zealand as well as a few Argentinians and Nigerians. The Worcester club began in the seventies and some of the old boys were still board members. No one cared that I was a Puerto Rican ex-gang member; they only cared about two things: that I played hard and drank hard.

After every game, the home team treats the visiting team to food and drink at a local pub, a tradition called the "drink up." With a pint in hand, all unsettled scores were forgotten or at least resolved quickly; we were to leave all our bickering and nonsense on the pitch. The drink up helped cement the social bonds of the group and to create our own little culture within the broader New England culture. It was where

I started to feel a real sense of camaraderie for the first time in my life.

I gave my time, energy, and body to the sport, and in turn it gave me a community and an escape from dissatisfaction at work and my broken heart. The only cost was that I was regressing into some kind of frat boy rather than progressing into a healthy, independent adult. Most of the dudes were young guys with no responsibilities. They lived in crappy apartments, smoked pot all day, chased girls all night, and worked part-time jobs to cover their bare necessities. I admired their lifestyles, believing them to be truly free.

Part of me was regressing, anyway. Another part of me was learning what it meant to not only participate in but eventually to help lead a 30-odd-year-old institution with national championships under its belt. My gregariousness and energy earned me a shared spot as Social Chairman for the club, meaning my co-chair and I had to organize all the planning for drink ups and social events. The club was a legit nonprofit, and I got to learn about it from the inside as well as use my position to get to know many area bar owners, bartenders, and business owners in addition to the college-aged kids who just loved to party after an afternoon of beating each other senseless. All I had to do to succeed was be my normal friendly self—and have a drink in my hand at all times.

One Way Off the Merry-Go-Round

April 14, 2008. I missed my exit heading home and pulled off at the next one, which took me through some dinky town named Sturbridge. I was pulled over and hit with a criminal charge for driving with a broken plate light. It meant yet another violation of probation plus an added year of probation on top of that. For kicks, they through in a $625 fine and a 60-day license suspension. I had to laugh at how every time I got close to getting out of one hole, I dug myself into another.

Throughout this period of building my glass house, I had been routinely failing to get off probation. It felt like I spent as much time with my probation officer or in a courtroom as I did with Monica. A guy like me, with my record, rarely got away from the most mundane traffic stop in the good commonwealth of Massachusetts without getting some stupid charge thrown at me. It was like, once you're in the system, they do their damnedest to keep you in.

May 14, 2008. I was pulled over in Framingham and dinged for driving with a suspended license. They towed my car but let me get a cab home rather than take me in. I guess that was being nice? Problem was, I couldn't get to work without driving, and if I couldn't get to work, I couldn't pay for rent or food much less my fines and court fees. What was I supposed to do?

July 30, 2008. I tried to merge into traffic from a highway offramp, missed one opportunity, then slipped in behind that guy and noticed that he was a cop. For his part, he noticed that I was shining my high beams in his mirror, and he did not care for it. He pulled me over and did not think I was clever for using my high beams to disguise my broken headlight. I received two extra criminal charges (beyond driving with a suspended license, of course), and my car received a trip to the impound. They wanted a buck-fifty to get it back, with a $75-per-day fee until I did.

This was a not-unfamiliar situation for a guy from the ghetto. Get in trouble, lose your license, drive anyway so you can get to work, get in trouble for driving without a license, drive to work anyway so you can pay your fines, get in trouble again, and so on. It's like being on a merry-go-round where you can't get off until they stop it, but they won't stop it as long as you're on it. I might have been reckless, especially to not take better care of my car, but I couldn't help but credit it to bad luck. On any given street there are at least a handful of people driving illegally or with drugs or weapons. My boy Ricky was often one of them, but he never seemed to attract negative attention like I did just for driving home from work.

On an ordinary court day, I sat in the crowded room and judged the hell out of all the drug addicts, petty criminals, gang members, baby mamas, and others who'd given up on life rather than try to make something of themselves like I had. This was in Dudley District Court, where I had to address one of my many probation violations. I wore my work clothes so I could head back as soon as I was done.

The Honorable Judge Snider sat on the bench that day, and I'll never forget the growing concern and surprise on his face as the DA listed my many violations. She concluded by recommending I be detained until my next court hearing. I thought she was crazy, but Judge Snider did not, and I didn't exactly have anything to offer in my defense. The gavel came down, and the court deputy walked over to me, reaching for his cuffs. I hadn't realized until that moment that it hadn't all been bad luck. For over a decade, I'd been given second, third, and twentieth chances. Now they were all used up. I was loaded onto a transport van and sent away to Worcester County Correctional for 18 days.

But don't think this was rock bottom for me. Oh, no, this was just a jagged outcropping on the way down to rock bottom. I did my time quietly and got out after my next hearing, swearing to myself that I'd never wind up back in there. Jack took me back, but he couldn't hide his disappointment. Actually, he reminded me how often he'd warned me about this happening, how he'd tried to get me on a different path. He told me again how I was screwing up my life and squandering all my potential.

I viewed Jack as a mentor, yes, but more in the way that a basketball star is a mentor, someone whose actions I watched, learned from, and imitated. When he interacted with others, I admired his intelligence, wit, and authority. He lived a life I dreamed of also living. Yet, I had a hard time taking direct advice from him. Monica had never liked him, which didn't help, and then I could never tell when he spoke to me whether he was really thinking about me or just trying to get more money for the company.

A couple bad incidents eroded my trust with upper management, too. First, I was falsely accused of stealing. I knew who had really done it, but my word held less weight with them than the air that carried it. Not long later, I was once again falsely accused, this time of listing another collector's debt under my collector number. The worst part was that the manager did it in front of the whole collection floor.

Jack had been a solid, straight-shooting, tough-love sort of guy in my life. He had seen me for more than the list of crimes pinned to my chest, and he had given me a career that I could dedicate myself to, but these betrayals coupled with Jack's palpable disappointment made me realize my time with them was running out. At the end of the day, I was only as good to Jack as the money I was making the business. When push came to shove and there was nothing more we could offer each other, I took matter into my own hands, I told him I wanted out. Then I saw his true colors come out. Realizing I would soon be beyond his mind control powers and probably genuinely hurt at the thought of losing me, he—like so many others before him—got ugly.

"Where the hell you gonna go, Carlos?" he complained, instantly agitated. "You'll never earn as much as you earn here. You're a felon with a criminal record longer than a dictionary. No one's going to hire you! I'm letting you know now: You're making a big mistake. If you quit, you'll end up as a grocery bagger or a cashier back at the convenience store.

You won't amount to sh** after this place. This is the best you're ever going to have in your life! Don't be stupid. Think about what you're doing, because I won't give you another chance to come back here once you're gone."

His words played on my every insecurity and fear like a master pianist. He knew exactly what to say to scare me into doing what he wanted—and he seemed to know he had me over a barrel. This was one of the few times I was thankful my anger kicked in to defend me. He had overstepped by playing all his cards at once, and that shocked me into reacting rather than simply being manipulated. Corner a mad dog like me and you're going to get bit. I went ahead and let him know a few of the things that had been on my mind about him.

Then I packed my things, said my goodbyes, and exited the building, vowing once again to never look back. I had fought and survived in another harsh environment, and now I would have to blow somewhere else. It felt like the right move, but I was also feeling tired of the fighting and surviving and remaking myself to fit whatever new place I found myself in. I couldn't see staying there any longer, but what if Jack was right? What if I just threw away the best job I'd ever have?

CONVERSATION WITH GOD

Here's the funny thing about quitting: It was my therapist's idea; it was supposed to free me from something toxic so I could pursue something more fulfilling.

Yeah, I had a therapist. I'd started seeing her just a couple weeks before the Halloween incident. Not long before that, I had failed random drug screening by my P.O. and was scared to death of what that might mean for me. Whatever it was, my dumb ass deserved it, but for all my screw ups, I had never shown up dirty on a random urine test before. It showed me just how far I had fallen from the respectable life I thought I was living. I had risked going to jail just for a little weed. What kind of loser didn't care enough about his life to take even that small precaution?

I walked out of the courthouse that day with a sunken feeling in my heart and ashamed of myself for being so dumb, lazy, and irresponsible. On the way to the car, I suddenly stopped, looked around a moment, then looked to the sky and—before I could think about what I was doing—said, "*Help!* I need help, God. I need to see a psychiatrist. I can't do this anymore." Then I went to work, found a local clinic, and booked myself an appointment.

Dr. Raine was a short and pudgy middle-aged woman with shoulder length hair who wore reading glasses on the tip of her nose and clothes that never left the pinnacle of her youth. During our first appointment, she set right to work breaking down the walls I had built up over years of emotional suffering. It was up to me to slowly work toward believing that, if I opened myself up, I'd succeed in finding the change

I had come to therapy looking for. Fortunately, I was motivated and she was a true professional. I was extremely candid with her regarding my concerns about therapy and my goals, and then over the course of several sessions I released a flood of unprocessed fears, worries, guilts, destructive thought patterns, and traumas. It got to where I would sit down on the couch and almost immediately begin weeping.

Dr. Raine showed me that not looking back was not the same as processing past problems—not by a longshot. She also helped me see how so much of my past traumas came back eventually to Mom. After listening to my long tale of woe, she pointed out that my life with Mom had been so unpredictable, violent, and even scary that I couldn't differentiate between normal and acceptable behavior and abnormal, self-destructive behavior.

I learned a lot about the self-destructive mind. The self-destructive mind cannot perceive the difference between a calculated risk and straight-up stupid. It refused to believe you will suffer criminal consequences for your actions no matter how many times it's been proven wrong. In fact, it convinces you you are above the law—the law is only a guideline, anyway.

It hates to be alone. It will drive you to all sorts of unhealthy and illegal behaviors so long as you don't have to be alone. It does not let you take responsibility for your actions, so you wrack up arrests and debts like it's a hobby of yours. And it cannot stand to think about the future or even really about the present, so it will drive you to drugs, booze, sex, or even your rugby mates or friends if they help you avoid reality.

The self-destructive mind obsesses over image and neglects character. It reacts based on emotion rather than values. It recruits your fear, starves your talents, and holds the best of you hostage so the worst of you can steal the spotlight.

All this became clear to me as we mined the layers of my psyche and started calling a lot of it what it was rather than shrugging it off as just my dumb luck.

Then one day she asked me, "Why are you afraid of success, Carlos?"

I looked at her, unsure how to respond. "What do you mean? Who's afraid of succeeding? It doesn't make sense," I said.

"You're afraid of success," she repeated. "You don't think you're worth it. You live your life sabotaging your own success because you feel that your failures are bigger than what you can achieve."

I gave it some serious thought, then reviewed all the factors working against me: "What am I supposed to do? I can't quit my job because I have bills to pay and I can't get a job anywhere else. I got a car payment that's almost $400 and insurance that's not much less. I can't go to school because I can't get financial aid with felonies on my record. I take pills to sleep and pump coffee and energy drinks into my system to stay awake at work, and meanwhile my brain works against me. Sometimes I feel like the smartest idiot in the room. My mom should've never had kids. I'm lucky to be alive and free rather than dead or in jail. I'm afraid of success because I spent my entire life failing and am tired of starting over again because of having failed over and over again."

It had taken me a minute to get there, but I eventually said it: I was afraid of success. She smirked a little, then said matter-of-factly, "You need to quit your job, got to school, and get a degree in literature, political science, journalism, or anything else that interests you. The life you're living isn't helping you get better. Rugby is a great hobby and outlet for you, but drinking isn't—especially with your background. Being that you're still on probation and still disregard the conditions you're given, you carelessly put your freedom on the line every day."

She was really only repeating back to me what I had already been telling her for weeks, but now I felt and seen in a way that hit me hard. She had only held a mirror up to me, but it felt like a spotlight, and what I saw was a man spreading himself thin trying to become someone he didn't want to be while trying to avoid dealing with the unhealthy parts of who he had been. I needed to better understand my brain and the sources of my anger so that I could stop cycling on self-destructive behaviors and start building a solid house on a solid foundation. As we continued to work together, it became easier to imagine making changes like leaving my job to free me up for better things.

I couldn't find solid ground to stand on, though, in order to start climbing toward those better things. Instead, my self-destructive mind nudged me closer and closer to the edge of the cliff. At this point I was sharing an apartment with some teammates from the rugby league. Jack had told me it was a bad idea to move in with them, but I hadn't listened, and now I wished I had. I didn't really know these people, and what I did know I didn't care much for. My car got totaled after a drug-fueled night with an ex-girlfriend's brother, so I had to stand in the cold for the bus to get to my monthly meetings with my probation officer. You could say I was falling apart, but that would imply there was any more "apart" to fall. I was already in pieces; it was just too painful to admit.

My pride didn't take well to these helpings of humble pie. I held onto my pride as long as I could. In the middle of winter I would be standing at the bus stop freezing my ass off because I was dressed like I was waiting for the valet to pull around my Mercedes. The one thing I could control was how I presented myself to the world, right? My pride would puff itself up and say to me, "Hey, you've been here before and got out, so you can do it again. Anyway, you got yourself into this mess; it's up to you to get yourself out."

In other words, I wasn't going down without a fight. I did whatever I could to hack it until tax season, when I expected a refund. For starters, I borrowed some money from Mom, who was dating a very well-off guy at the time. She also gave me a run-down minivan for getting around, which would have been nicer if it hadn't had more repair needs than Humpty Dumpty.

Then I looked for work at a restaurant or bar. Application after application went nowhere. Besides having no experience, I had, of course, my record. When things got desperate, I reverted to my old gig: selling weed. I wasn't going to let something like the law get in the way of my survival, after all. I would have made more money doing that if I hadn't smoked more than I sold. That was Rule Number Two in *Scarface*: "Don't get high on your own supply." But I had been too distracted by the parties and the mansions to really take to heart the moral of that film. Besides, I was Puerto Rican, not Cuban.

Things were not looking good. I filed my taxes early and got a refund, but by Valentine's Day I had burned through everything except my last few hundred bucks. If I didn't find a job soon, I'd be looking at eviction and homelessness again. I needed to get serious.

Instead, I bought some Valentine's Day-themed red and white clothes and some fresh new kicks, got a tight fade at the barber shop, and headed to a party where I hoped to hook up again with some random chick I'd slept with at a party a few weeks prior. I could hear my therapist's voice in my head, calmly telling me all the things I already knew and encouraging me to believe in myself, but where she was talking softly, my self-destructive mind was shouting, "Blaze of glory! Blaze of glory!"

To my chagrin, the chick blew me off all night; she had her hips set on some other dude. Instead of shaking it off, I kept pouring alcohol on my irritation, until finally I said screw it, grabbed a couple rookie teammates, and suggested it was time to leave this lame party and find some place to chill at and grub.

This was around three in the morning. All three of us were drunk, and I was driving us to Wings Over Worcester, the only place around open late and worth eating at. As we pulled up, we noticed three Puerto Rican guys chilling outside. I tensed up; this late at night, anything might happen when you get a bunch of drunk guys huddled together at the same location. Over wings, of all things, too.

We get out of the car and go to enter the restaurant, but this guy steps in front me who's skinny as a toothpick and has a crazy look in his eyes.

"I know you," he says. "You're a Blood. Yeah, you're a Blood."

My buddies, two white civilians—that is, not members of the Kings, Bloods, or any other street gang—looked confused, but I assured them this guy had me confused with someone else, because obviously he had. I tried to sidestep the guy, but he blocked me again and then called to his two boys over at the picnic table, "Hey, this guy's a Blood. He lying to me."

"I do know you," he told me. "I'm a Latin King, and you ain't going nowhere."

Still trying to avoid any escalation, I looked him dead in the face and made it clear that he'd confused me with someone else, that I didn't know him or his friends. I told him my name and that I thought he'd better get out of my way before I got him out.

We were all too drunk to be getting into anything, but that was exactly why we were getting into something. Again, we were at a chicken wing restaurant, of all places; this was not from the *Scarface* playbook.

The two guys behind Mr. Toothpick started to come around, and while I watched them, Mr. Toothpick himself clocks his arm back to punch me. My boxing reflexes kicked in. I ducked and came up with a solid punch to his face that might have ended a one-on-one, but one of his compatriots caught me on the side of the head. I fell back a few steps and called for my teammates for help, but they stayed behind me with utter terror on their faces. One of them was big enough to pin two guys just by falling on them, but it's always the size of the fight in the dog that counts in these situations.

I shook my head in disappointment, disbelief, and the absurd realization that I was somehow in this alone, just like so many other situations in my life. With a quick movement, I pulled out a pocket knife that I carried for emergency repairs in the minivan.

"What you gonna do now, huh? What you gonna do?" I taunted.

"Yeah, man, you ain't gonna use that. Sh**," said Toothpick.

"Why you backing up, then, huh? If I'm not gonna use it?" I said. "Come here. Come closer if you don't think I'm gonna use it, pendejo!"

His two friends scurried around the parking lot looking for weapons. One of them found a large rock and the other a long stick. Toothpick took courage from this and started coming toward me. Instinctively (so it seemed), I swing quickly at his abdomen with my right hand.

"Ahhhh! You f*****g stabbed me, motherf****r!" he screamed, and I realized it was true.

Everything seemed to be happening very quickly to my inebriated mind. Toothpick was screaming, his buddies were confused and shocked, and then suddenly something grabbed me from behind, threw me to the ground, and pinned me there with his knees. I fought back, of course, not realizing until a moment later that it was a Worcester cop. The fight went out of me and I began to cooperate. The last thing I needed was another run-in with the law, but truth be told,

I was also glad they'd stopped us before I wound up killing somebody.

The next thing I knew—literally; I have no memory of the arrest or drive to the station—I was sitting inside a small records room beside a filing cabinet. A detective began to ask me about what happened, and I told him as truthfully as I could muster. They took my blood-splattered pants and shoes as evidence, so when they finally booked me, I had to hold up oversized shorts like some crazy person they'd pulled off the streets. From there, I was sent back to county lockup, the same place I'd promised myself I'd never return to. Here, at last, on a unit called K Block, I'd be broken enough that God could finally reach me.

No More Tomorrow

I used to tell myself, when I was about to do something stupid I had told myself I wouldn't do again, that I'd change things the next day. "There's always tomorrow," I'd think. This one last time won't kill me, and tomorrow I'll start fresh. Tomorrow, I'll stop hanging out with the wrong crowd, say no to my friends, obey the law, pay my court fines, do my community service, stop lying to myself, and put my life in order. Well, looking down the long row of cells that would become my new home, it didn't feel like there was a tomorrow anymore.

Tomorrow, I'd wake up in the same 8' x 12' room with the same cold steel toilet and the same stranger for a cellmate. We'd do the same things we did today and the day before. I had become a statistic, the immigrant, single-parent, street-raised, impoverished, gang-banging, drug-dealing, dope-smoking criminal that Ms. DeVille had warned I would become. I entered prison feeling like I didn't belong among society's rejected, dejected, and deplorable, but as a storm of depression and anxiety overcame me, it was harder and harder not to feel like that was exactly where I belonged. My life would consist of frequent stays in prison followed by a life of dead-end jobs, government assistance, child support payments, and generally seeing anything I worked for squandered before I could much enjoy it.

I tortured myself with thoughts of all those Ms. DeVilles who just knew I was no good. I imagined their smug satisfaction at having seen the future so clearly. I heard the laughter of old classmates and bosses who'd always known I wasn't so smart and talented. I imagined Laura discovering that her brother, after nearly five years of turning his life around, was now rotting in a prison cell. I plagued myself picturing Monica triumphantly vindicated for having left me.

After about two weeks of mental and emotional turmoil, something unexpected happened. I became light as a feather and carefree as a child. My old life was gone—and I mean gone. Going back to Jack or Monica was out of the question. And I didn't care so much about any of my possessions; those had long since lost their luster. That meant that for the first time in a long time, I had nothing to sustain and nothing to lose. No monthly goals to meet, no external images to maintain one way at work and another at church. No more bills, no rent, no constant fear that someone would learn of my criminal background. No more stealing groceries when I didn't have enough money to eat. No more excuses to the landlord, no more lies to Monica about how great my life was. I could breathe stress-free because I didn't have to tiptoe around my glass house anymore. I could sleep easy at night because this resurrection plant had blown into a place where, if it didn't rain enough for me to bloom, it was at least required to keep me alive.

In my world, I had done the impossible. I had risen above the streets. The irony, of course, was that I'd discovered that not all that glitters is gold. Just as ironically, my life had been something like a merciful version of *Scarface*, one of the key templates for the gangsta life. I hadn't risen so high, but that meant I didn't have to fall quite so hard, which in turn meant that I might be able to get up again.

Life did go on, in its way. When Mom and her rich boyfriend caught wind of what had happened to me, they hired an attorney from Boston to work on reducing my charges. This time they were Felony Assault & Battery with a Dangerous Weapon (Knife), Misdemeanor Resisting Arrest (the guy jacked me from behind *in a fight*, but whatever), and Misdemeanor Disorderly Conduct. If I was lucky, they might reduce the felony to a misdemeanor. More likely, it would be my third felony and nineteenth criminal offense. Quite the bragging rights for my boys back in the hood, huh?

Of all my old teammates and party-going friends, only a handful of people bothered writing to me in prison, which forced upon me the sobering realization of how skin-deep those relationships were. Meanwhile, on the inside, the Latin Kings who had been there a while took care of me. I welcomed the built-in social network, but I knew they were just like the guys on the outside, high most of the time and capable of betraying you if it served their purposes.

Between the down time and the isolation, prison gives you a lot of time for reflection, if you'll take it. Hindsight had never been 20/20 for me because I'd always been too hardheaded to look back—at least, not during the times when my head was on straight enough to see clearly. The problem with looking back at a life like mine, though, is that it's depressing. But where my usual depression came out of and led back to self-destructive thoughts and behaviors, the depression of seeing how badly I'd broken my life was more existential. It was tied up with a grief at realizing that some things might not be fixable and that I was no longer in control of most of my life. It was a depression that came from knowing that I had to give up some things I thought were important, like my pride, in order to really turn my life around.

Now that it was just me, myself, and God, I was finally ready to take this moment of clarity seriously. I was ready to hang up the gloves and stop fighting, to man up and take responsibility for what I had become, to humble myself and repent, and to seek help from the one source that had never given up on me: God.

A One-on-One with the Big Man

God and I had been on rough terms for a while, now. I had tried so hard to live a good life, and as it fell apart around me, I blamed God for giving me false hope. I felt like God had taken an inordinate interest in making my life more miserable and tragic than it would be anyway if He had just left me alone. I didn't have anywhere else to turn, though.

So one night, long after the cell block lights went out and shortly after I sensed my bunky was well into his dreams, I turned back to God for a much-needed one-on-one.

Normally when I prayed, I addressed God as I would an elder for whom I had deep respect and reverence. This time, however, there was no question of impressing Him with my deeds of the week or my formal language. I was defeated, raising my arms in surrender, done clinging to my piss-poor attempts at salvaging a decaying life. I walked through a list of complaints and grievances going back a long way. I let out all the things I resented and blamed Mom for. I asked why He made me someone unable to lie, which meant I got into all sorts of trouble my friends talked their way out of. I asked why He made me so empathic and kindhearted when the world just stepped all over people like that. I asked why He let things with Monica go the way they had.

I literally spoke these prayers out loud, or in a low mumble under my breath, anyway, and I had the powerful sense of a presence lying beside me the whole time. And something like a voice, only coming from deep within me, responded to my questions and prompted me. It was like I was lying in bed beside Monica, only better, just having a conversation.

There was no grand revelation, no shining light or burning bush. Many times I would repeat back what I'd heard as if I wasn't sure, though I was really just stalling as I considered what I had to do next. More often than not, my complaints would lead to recognitions of my own guilty behavior and thus to confession. More than anything else that night, I confessed to all the crap I'd done and how cold and heartless I'd been during my street days when so much seemed justifiable as a means of survival. I was direct, specific, and contrite, and I asked for help making the deep-down change I needed.

This went on for two or three hours; I didn't know for sure other than that we had covered a lot of ground. When I had unloaded all the horrible stuff that I had let define me, I felt a growing sense of gratitude. I began to thank God for that time together and then for every good thing I had experienced from childhood until then. I thanked Him for the bad things that I actually learned from, or at least that I had grown from many of them. I found myself thanking him for Mom and for the good years with Ralph, while they lasted. I thanked Him for Laura, someone I could love as a child and who inspired me to be a better example.

The life I had lived was rough, chaotic, and traumatic, but alongside all the hardships I had managed to find joy in life. I tasted both the bitter and the sweet, doing things my way, which sometimes meant standing out from the crowd. Through it all, as dark as things got, something inside me never stopped telling me I had more living left to do.

At last, I felt myself needing to sleep, so I took a deep breath and asked God what I needed to do for my life to change. Immediately, as if He had been waiting for this question all along, I heard my friend Max's voice: *You don't love yourself enough to change, Carlos.*

Max and Emmy were old neighbors of mine. We'd gotten pretty close, or at least they were kind enough to let me hang out with them and unburden my soul to them from time to time about my adventures of the week. I had a lot of unburdening to do in the weeks and months after Monica broke it off with me for good. On one such night, I had been whining along the lines of, "Why can't I stop thinking about her, Max? I miss her. I feel like without her I can't get my life together again. She was too good for me, and I knew it from the beginning but didn't wanna believe it. It's like she was the Virgin Mary and I was this scumbag who came into her life to ruin it. You know how I'm living, now. I don't have a care for what happens to me or where I end up, bro. Why do I live like this? Why can't I stop? It's crazy!"

Max looked at me kindly and said, "Can I be honest with you, Carlos?"

"Of course, dude, come on," I assured him. "It's *me* you're talking to, here."

"Alright. To be honest with you, it's because you don't love yourself enough to change, Carlos," he replied bluntly.

At the time I couldn't really process it. Love myself? You see how I'm dressed, bro? You know how hard I work to get what I got? Tell me I don't love myself! But some part of me cataloged and stored it as good advice I would understand later so I should hang onto it. It didn't even dawn on me how similar his words were to Dr. Raine calling me out for being afraid of success. And now God Himself was pulling that little Post-It out of a box of old memories.

Still, I stalled. "Love myself?" I said. "That's what you want me to do?"

Yes, came the reply.

"But what does that mean, God? Because if I don't do that already, then it means I've been doing it all wrong."

I thought of all my broken relationships, most of which had been broken by my own actions.

"I guess it's true I don't know how to properly love someone, and they say you have to love yourself, first. So, if You want me to love myself, tell me how I start doing that."

An image appeared in my mind of looking in a mirror, and the voice told me to wake up the next morning and look at myself in the mirror, and to do it again the next day and every day thereafter until I started to accept myself for everything I was. It still confused me. Why did I need to accept the guy in the mirror when everything about my look and my way of walking and talking had been crafted by me? Despite all my impatience with others' hypocrisy and phoniness, I couldn't see how I, too, wore masks.

"How do I do that, Father? How in the world do I start doing something so hard to understand and that I've apparently been wrong my whole life?"

Once again, the voice immediately responded.

Accept your nose. Accept your lips. Accept your face. Accept your flaws, your imperfections. Accept your past and your pain. Accept your father, your mother. Accept your failures and your fears. Accept who you are. Accept yourself for everything you've tried to change and for everyone you've spent your life trying to become. Accept everything about your life. Forgiveness is the way to acceptance and acceptance is the way to peace. When you do that and begin to love yourself for it, you will truly begin to feel as if your existence on this earth was meant for something greater that what you've ever thought possible.

It was so specific and so total, and it was not about whether I was accepted by anybody else but myself. It felt like an invitation to come home and rest—if only I could scale this large mountain, first.

Then the voice continued with a different list: *Stop chasing money. Stop chasing girls. Stop chasing your image, trying to be hard, trying to impress everyone. Stop acting like everything is okay when it's not. Stop making bad friendships. Stop being so angry. Stop being so careless with your blessings and feeling like the world is out to get you. Stop running from your past. Stop putting loyalty to others over your own safety and saying yes to every bad idea. And stop feeling inferior to those who have more than you. Once you do these things, everything will start changing.*

The mountain was made of these things, too, but I didn't hear them as more things I needed to. Quite the reverse. All the things I had to stop doing were things that were keeping me down, stressing me out, and hurting me. To stop them would mean to become free of them.

God had spoken to me in my own voice and in Max's voice, and now He spoke to me in the voice of a former rugby teammate: "You know what your problem is, Carlos? You don't take any responsibility for the things you do. You always blame someone or something else for it."

I let those words sink in for a bit. *You don't take any responsibility.* I repeated them over and over in my head until I grasped their significance. I always told myself that I made my own choices, but it was true I always blamed others for the bad things that happened to me. Often, a series of things put pressure on me until I reacted to them. My life was a Jenga tower I knew would tumble at any time, so I would finally decide if anyone was going to knock it over, it was damn certain going to be me. Even then I would feel like I'd been backed into a corner and forced to act like I did.

But this time I knew I'd gotten myself here and had no one to blame. Truthfully, I was so tired of that old life that if taking responsibility meant a step in the right direction, then it'd be entirely my fault if I *didn't* do it and give myself the chance for a better life.

"I guess that's it, huh? Just a laundry list of 180-degree turns to execute. No biggie, God," I prayed, then drifted off to sleep.

ZIG ZAG ZIG

That conversation marks a turning point in my life. After that, I had a new sense of purpose, a new appreciation for who I was and what I could become. I had let go of the guilt and anger that had weighed me down, I had lowered the mask of pride and ego. None of that stuff had helped me find love; it had actually blocked me from it.

This is the part in the movie when the hero marches like a terminator bot up the hill he'd been falling down the whole time and finally conquers it. It makes for an inspiring story and helps wrap things up, but it's not how life has ever worked for me. I'd zigged and zagged up that hill of success and fallen back down only to find it was the wrong hill or the wrong path up or whatever spin you want to put on that metaphor.

Spending an hour or two talking to God changed my heart, but it didn't completely overhaul my life overnight. I had my marching orders, but it would take months and years to carry them out. As much as I'd like to rush to the part when I finally got my life together and could turn around to write this book, that wouldn't feel honest. Nor would it help the people I most hope to help with my story, the people who will have to zig and zag and zig in their own lives before things will get better. The resurrection plant has to get blown around *a lot*, gathering what little nourishment it can wherever it goes, until it finds a place that can sustain it—if it ever does.

It's not much of a spoiler to say I did eventually find that place, but first I had to survive another few months of prison and then return to what little was left of my life on the outside. I woke up the morning after that prayer feeling refreshed, hopeful, and driven. Though I was in prison, surrounded by wolves and vultures ready to hunt me and eat me, dead or alive, I felt positive about my ability to start tackling my heavenly punch list. The work I needed to do was internal, and I just happened to have few external responsibilities to distract me from it.

Self-improvement replaced self-preservation as my central motivation. I began to seek out interactions with people where I could learn what really made them tick, how they wound up where they were, what they really wanted out of life. I stopped being so confrontational (like everyone else) and tried to become someone you could have a conversation with and who could maybe help you see things in a different light. I wanted to see if my new approach to life could help others, too.

Meanwhile, I began to take stock of myself, almost to observe myself the way I did other people. What made me tick? What did I like and dislike? What made me angry or sad, what might trigger me to want to get aggressive? Why did I say that thing to that guy? Between my new perspective and this self-reflection process, I started to distinguish real differences in the new me compared with the old me. Because I respected myself enough to discipline myself, I could act more like the person I wanted to be and less like the person everyone expected me to be.

The single biggest shift came in the way I defined my value. It was no longer about my clothes or shoes or car or girl. It wasn't about my music or the money I made. It was about me as a person, my character, my ethics, the things I carried inside myself that no one could take away. No became no, yes became yes. I started to shrug or laugh off things that used to put me in a fighting mood. I worked to find the positive rather than assume the negative.

Here's the thing about prison, though: If you're a Latin King on the outside, you're a Latin King on the inside. The perks of membership—notably, protection—become even more important in the pressure cooker of a cell block. Now, I accepted the protection because it was useful, but I was ambivalent at best about the Nation. The guys I'd run with turned snitch or, in King Fear's case, had been governmental informants all along. In my earlier 18-day stint at County, I'd seen how the Kings inside were doped up all the time and spent an awful lot of time double-crossing each other. Affiliation with them was only marginally better than nothing.

Not long after my conversation with God, they transferred me to another block. That meant I would have to do all that work over again of establishing my reputation, but at least I could connect up with that block's Latin Kings as a start. I couldn't imagine what would actually happen, nor realize until later that it was in fact a God thing.

It may sound funny to hear this, because the thing that happened was my new cellmate was the Inca, or leader, of the Latin Kings in the entire facility. I always sought out mentors to help me navigate my world, and there was no more powerful mentor in prison than the Inca.

They called him Bino, short for Gambino, and he got right to the point.

"I couldn't stand my last bunky," he told me after I'd been dropped off in my new cell. "There were no other cells to transfer him to, so I had him check himself out. Don't be next."

By "check himself out," Bino meant his old cellmate had requested protected custody, or PC, in order to be moved somewhere else. The suggestion that one request PC was enough reason to believe you really needed it.

"A'ight, cool," I replied, keeping calm. "I'm Carlos. You can call me Los or Loso, whatever you want."

"This is a King room. If you got a problem with that, then get the f*** out. The CO's coming by in another 20 minutes. You could check yourself then."

Almost reflexively, I said, "*ADR, hermanito.*" He stood up, so I hopped down from my bunk, stood before him, and initiated the King salute. He then asked me for my points, which I gave, and then he started grilling me about my background, which Latin Kings chapter I was from, and questions about King activity and lore. To be honest, I was nervous as hell. I didn't have a lot of King knowledge, so I didn't know whether my responses were making this guy trust me or suspect me or whether he might suddenly snap and come after me.

Thankfully, he understood that King Fear had run an undisciplined and unrighteous chapter in Lowell—shoot, he was a rat, after all. Bino approved of my responses and, in no time at all, took me under his wing. We shared that cell for another eight weeks, and in that time he not only mentored me in the ways of leadership (in his way) but told me story upon story about the Nation—he was a walking Latin King encyclopedia.

Bino was in his 40s, came from Florida, had lived a long life of drug dealing, drug abusing, and gang living. He could talk for days, had jokes for weeks and stories for years. He responded to my intelligence and maturity, and I think it gave him some sense of pride and purpose to adopt me as his second-in-command and protégé.

"Lions never hunt," he once told me. "Their job is to protect and defend the pride. Lionesses and cubs hunt. They're the ones you send out to get the job done. You and I will never put our positions in jeopardy because once the head of the snake is gone, the body still moves but it has no sense of direction and eventually dies."

In other words, I could be an extra set of eyes and ears and an advisor, but the other brothers were the enforcers. That didn't mean Bino couldn't get ugly and scary. He wasn't a big guy, but he could make the biggest, baddest dude in the whole jail shake at his approach. In other words, his power came from his reputation and the loyalty he created in others more than in his physical ability to personally kick your ass.

Once, Bino, a fellow brother, and I had a Puerto Rican kid cornered in an empty cell. Bino got up in his face.

"You reppin' King around here but don't know your points or the holy prayer, and you talking to one of our hermanitos about the Nation, then lied to me that you ever said you were a brother?" he snarled. "*I* run the nation in this jail. *Me!* I'm the Inca, here. I could have you torn apart right now. Why shouldn't I have my lions bang you up right here?"

As far as I could tell, the kid was literally crapping his pants at this point.

Then Bino said, "Listen, here's what I'm gonna do. I'm not gonna send my lions after you. I'm gonna have mercy on you. But if I hear you speak the word *King* or even talk about the Nation in any way, they coming after you wherever you at."

The judgment had been made prior to us catching this kid; this was just a sentencing. Bino continued, "You can no longer live here, son. Once we get back in our rooms, check yourself out to PC. I don't wanna see your face on this block again."

And that's what he did; we never saw him again. I thought it a rather light consequence, since most punks like him would be taught a lesson, so I asked Bino why he let him go.

"One thing you gotta learn is mercy—and when to have it," he replied. "If you show mercy to people, you own them for life; they owe you. You let them off the hook, and now they're in your pocket forever. I notice how quick you are to get hype sometimes, Los. You gotta learn to have mercy. Someone, somewhere in your past, had mercy on you, and someone will again down the road. If you learn how and when to be merciful, you'll eliminate a lot of unnecessary problems in life—and life will be merciful back."

Call it God's sense of humor or His mysterious ways or what have you, but this was a powerful lesson for me. I'd been ready to quietly nod my head while Bino's "lion" helped that poor Rican kid to mind his p's and q's with a few jabs to the gut, and here I learned that sometimes being powerful meant *not* beating the guy up. The more I thought about mercy, the more I learned to "let go and let God," as they said in church. I didn't have to respond to every little thing. In fact, doing so only got me a reputation as a hot head. And if God smacked me down for every one of my sins, I'd hardly ever be standing upright. It was His mercy that I was still alive to learn this lesson at all.

The jail's priest taught me another helpful lesson one day after our church service. I had told him how his message had hit home and described so much of my life, how I'd try so hard to make progress but kept finding myself in one problem after another.

"Any progress I've ever made," I told him, "there's been all sorts of bumps in the road, and obviously, now I'm here."

He looked at me, then at the floor. He put his feet on a tile and said, "Sometimes in life, you take three steps forward, then two steps back." He demonstrated by walking forward three tiles, then back two. "The key thing is to notice you've still gained an extra step beyond where you were. What's happened to *you*," he continued, returning to his original tile, "is that you've gone *two* steps forward, then *three* steps back." He demonstrated again, this time winding up behind his starting tile.

"If you start opening yourself to God's purpose for you and take notice of the steps you're taking in life, you'll not only see how far you've gone or how far you've fallen behind, you'll also start to appreciate any small progress after your stumbles."

He walked ahead one step and stopped. He was showing me that, even though he'd only gotten back to where he'd started, it was still a form of progress, it wasn't only backsliding.

"You'll never know what the devil will throw at you, but God will always be there to help you up if you let Him," he concluded.

I was used to feeling like the devil was knocking me down, but I hadn't understood that God was there to help rather than just watch and maybe laugh at me. He'd had to wait till I was in jail before I was receptive to that kind of thing. As I learned to let go of my anger and open myself to the changes God wanted me to make, though, the world around me began to make a bit more sense. God hadn't made me to live a life written out for me by my family or by the streets or even by my church; He'd made me to live my own life.

WHAT GOES UP—ON THE STREETS—MUST COME DOWN

Four months into my stay at Worcester County, Mom's boyfriend paid 10% of my bail of $10,000 as surety to the court. We were in Framingham district court to address one of my many open cases, and mercifully the DA agreed to give me time served on the charges and close the case then and there. It felt like the universe was making room for me to start my new lease on life with at least less baggage than I'd had the day before.

Not that the universe planned to make it easy. With no place else to go, I asked my attorney (hired by Mom's boyfriend) to drop me off at my old apartment. I wanted to see some familiar, friendly faces and at least find a couch to sleep on. Bo, an old teammate from Worcester Rugby Club, was mowing lawn, and when I stepped out of the car he did a double take. I looked every bit the felon I was: crazy hair, oversized orange jailhouse clothes, and a black garbage bag with what personal possessions I had. He welcomed me and started filling me in on some changes around the place— including the fact that now our friend Henry was staying in my old room.

Henry was a selfish, bitter, old-boy rugger from Kenya, a man in his 50s who had his own share of hardships and spent most of his day's drinking Foster's at the bar. He also had a grudge with me because we had competed to rent the same place and I'd won. When I went inside, Henry was sitting on the couch (*my* couch, incidentally). He watched me but didn't say anything right away as I rushed about the apartment to find that my things had been more or less ransacked. My stereo equipment had been stolen, as had most of my other gadgets. Clothes were missing, including socks and underwear (you know you live in a rough place when someone steals your underwear). Worst of all, my cat was nowhere to be found.

Bo and Henry looked stupidly guilty. I knew I'd learn nothing from them about what happened to my things. Chances were they genuinely didn't know. The fact that someone had taken my things bothered me less than the fact that these guys, who I'd thought were friends, didn't have my back.

"What about the cat?" I asked them, growing increasingly irritated with them.

"Bro," Bo started, and by the way he was shifting back and forth on his feet and avoiding eye contact I knew it wasn't going to be good, "she disappeared, like, months ago. We looked everywhere, you know, but we couldn't find her. She died, man; I'm sorry."

I'm not even a cat person, but I'd sort of inherited her and felt a responsibility to take care of her. She was super skittish and usually hid under the bed rather than run out the door.

"Died? How do you know? You found her?"

"Uh, yeah, man," Bo continued. "She, uh, got upstairs and got locked in the attic, and, uh, we didn't find her till she started to smell."

I couldn't handle it. The poor thing depended on us, and they just let her die and rot in a lonely attic. Not so different than they'd done to me. I didn't believe half their story—mostly the half that made it sound like they cared at all—and let them know it.

Then I had another problem: Where was I going to stay that night? Bo nodded sympathetically, but Henry looked me straight in the face and said, "You can't stay here. There's no room, here."

I couldn't believe this guy, but Bo was reluctant to step in.

"Well, it looks like you're sitting on my couch," I said, "which looks like a perfectly good spot for me to sleep in, tonight."

"Aw, man, I forgot this was your couch," Henry said. He moved to the smaller couch, but repeated his refusal. "As I was saying, unfortunately, you can't stay here. It's too crowded."

I was about done looking at his conceited, dismissive mug. Bo finally spoke up.

"Henry, he can stay for a night. He has nowhere else to go. I live here, too, and I'm fine with him staying for a night."

Henry didn't fight Bo on this but started muttering curses under his breath.

I looked at Bo and said, "It's all good, bro. I'll figure it out. Just let me into the basement to see what's left of my stuff."

So began several weeks of couch-bumming at friends' places. First, my friend Rod put me up, but after about two weeks I could tell he was getting tired of me. After Rod, I didn't have many options, so I called Betty, who lived an hour and a half away. She said she'd come pick me up.

Though Betty was a single mom of two, she had been homeless herself, so she had taken me in a couple times when I'd had fights with Mom. She treated me like her little brother and I saw her like an older sister. She never beat around the bush with me but always told me straight up what she thought. She was honest and down-to-earth and made me feel cared about but not judged. Whenever I stayed with her, she'd show me how you don't have to be a perfect parent to raise near-perfect kids, and how you can be happy just being yourself, flaws and all. This time around, I soaked those lessons in more than I ever had before.

I was proud to have a person like Betty in my life, and I did my best to show her how much I appreciated her, but I knew I couldn't stay with her forever, either. Without a job or prospects, no money, and no home, I told her what we'd both known was true for a long time: I'd have to go live down in Orlando with my mother.

Mom and her boyfriend helped me get down there and put me up on yet another couch. Seeing Mom after all she'd done for me made me feel like a little kid, again. It was humbling, but I also needed what little nurturing she could give me.

Mom was still Mom, though. She treated me like her little boy, still, and tried to control almost everything I did when I was home. It took very little time for me to remember all the bad things about living with Mom, having to walk on eggshells all the time lest you violate some rule you didn't even know existed. Life with Mom could be full of intense and happy highs, but more often it felt like a dungeon of alternating violence and depression.

I did my best to manage things at home while trying to build some kind of life in Orlando. Mom's old behaviors reinforced the idea that I really was on my own in this. In my old life, I would have let this realization get me down in the dumps, and then I'd mope about my room feeling sorry for myself and blaming the world for it. In my new life, all of that looked like an excuse to be lazy and sit around the house. I wanted to get past the dreaming and moping and blaming and get to doing something. So, I did.

I went out looking for work. Then I joined the Orlando Griffins Rugby Football Club. The more I got out in the world doing things, the better I felt about my life. I met new people and saw new environments that expanded my horizons. The process I began in prison of searching for the positive continued in "real life" even as I struggled with getting my feet under me and found myself in the vain world of sun-soaked Orlando. It wasn't always a pretty trek up the mountain, but I finally felt like I was gaining a step even after I fell backward.

Mac became my new mentor or model. Mac was a high school teacher and president of our rugby club. Like me, he was single, but unlike me he had a steady job and owned his own home. Since he made his way from Utah to Florida, he'd created a comfortable life for himself. More impressive to me, a New England street kid, was how positive, drama-free, and easy-going he was.

Mac introduced me to Mitch, who lived at Mac's place and happened to be Hulk Hogan's younger brother. He introduced me to other guys they knew. In short order, I became social director for the club, and I was hanging with Mac on at least a weekly basis. They didn't care how I dressed or how I talked; they just wanted to help out a fellow rugger.

I welcomed the new social group but couldn't help suspecting him. I'd never known anyone so willing to go out of his way to simply be a good friend to someone else. I couldn't even appreciate how sad that was, but I did respond to this new dynamic. These guys weren't constantly hiding their envy, judgment, wariness, or gossip; they were just chill and decent to each other. Over time, they wore me down, and I formed closer friends with these guys after a few weeks than I had in two years with the guys up north.

The other important mentor during this period was Mom's boyfriend. He'd spent a lot of money on me between the attorney and bail and court fees, but I never felt like he was holding it over me. Instead, he seemed to enjoy listening to me talk and sort of living vicariously through me. I felt like we understood each other, in part because, with his money and his disability, he had been taken advantage of and gone through a period of closing himself off to people. Now, we were both on a process of learning to open ourselves to the world again.

The Resurrection Plant

Sometimes we'd stay up late into the night just talking over Scotch and cigars. Or, rather, I would be talking and he would sit back and listen. He liked to say, "It's Carlos' brain-picking time," which I always found funny. Most of the time I would recount past experiences as a way to reflect on how I got myself into that situation in the first place—and how I could avoid doing it again. Occasionally, we'd get on even weightier topics like the existence and nature of God.

He'd been an atheist since an accident left him paraplegic at age 18; the same accident that led to a class action lawsuit and a sizable stipend for the rest of his life. He similarly rejected destiny or miracles. "If He or they existed, I'd be walking right now," he'd say. I would tell him stories from my own life to illustrate where I saw God preserving me and how He spoke with me that night in prison. He, in turn, would explain his theory of how the universe worked, which I still think about.

"If there's no God and nothing to look for, how do you not get depressed and hopeless?" I asked him once.

"I believe our thoughts do things," he said. "Our mindset matters, and what we put out in the world matter. You have to stay positive and do what good you can. That's why even people who appear put-together on the outside can live miserable lives inside. Having money isn't the important thing; you can wind up a wreck even with a lot of money. It's putting good out there and getting good back."

He told me about several people he'd met in the fancy social circles his money gave him access to, people who followed that pattern of looking like they had it all while being horrible people and generally winding up unhappy. He'd been on the path until some family members took advantage of him. It sent him into a suicidal spiral that took him some time to pull out of. After that, he wanted to live a different life and to believe the world was about more than just getting, getting, getting.

"Maybe I'm trying to prove there is a God without having to believe in one," he said.

The Scotch had greased the wheels of my mind a bit, and as I considered what he was saying, I tried to understand him in terms of his life and how he'd arrived at his way of thinking. The idea that it wasn't just our negative actions but our negative *thoughts* that could stunt our potential; it made a lot of sense. Suddenly, something shifted in my mind, and even without fully understanding what he was suggesting, I felt like I could see how and why he thought it. I was learning to think outside of myself.

Another time, we were sitting outside a Five Guys burger joint, waiting to go to a movie, and I asked him why he'd been so generous to me.

"Keep in mind," I added, before he could speak, "that one day I'll be in a position to pay you back. I promise, man."

He chuckled and reached out to touch my arm.

"You don't have to pay me back. I don't need the money, nor did I help you expecting something in return. I did it because you needed it and I was in a position to do it. That's all."

It was a good answer, but I could hardly understand what he was trying to say.

"But I feel a sense of obligation to pay you back," I told him. "No one's ever done what you've done for me—and without even knowing me."

"Listen," he said, "there are two things I'm going to tell you that I want from you in return."

"Yes, anything. Just let me know."

"If you and someone else fell off a boat without life vests, and the other person can't swim and starts drowning, how will you be able to save them without making sure you're safe first? You need to first make sure you can get to the safety of the boat before you can help the other person, right?"

I have to admit this confused me, at first. He was suddenly telling me some kind of children's fable or something, but I tried to go along with it.

"I guess? But why can't you just bring the person to safety with you?"

"You've now increased your chances of drowning and decreased your chances at surviving. You can't predict what that person will do, how frantic they'll get, how heavy they are, or if you've got the energy to get you both back. That's my point to you. You have to start looking at life like you're drowning. There's no way for you to survive if you haven't saved yourself, first. You'll never get ahead if you start giving and doing more for people and not have anything left to do or give to yourself. I know it sounds selfish, at first, but understand that, in life, everyone is out to survive, and some people do that by climbing on other people's backs, while other people never get ahead because they give more than they have to offer."

That all took a minute to digest. If you're a giver, then the takers are going to find you and keep taking as long as you give. That's what he was trying to tell me. Make sure you have what you need so you can give from your abundance and not from some false sense of heroism or virtue.

He continued, "Which leads me to the second thing. When you get to safety, the point in your life where you have the means to pay me back, I only ask one thing of you: I ask that you pay it forward. You know what means?"

"Yeah," I replied, "to give it to someone else rather than paying it back."

"Yes, but by paying it forward you're also paying me back. Do it for someone else, just remember that you can't help someone else unless you're in a position to help yourself, first. Help someone who is in a place you used to be. That's all I ask of you."

What Goes Up—On the Streets—Must Come Down

I'd come a long way from the streets of Lowell, where one of the first things I learned was not to take nothing from nobody lest they get the idea you're a pushover. Now, I was actually imagining a time when I would do something for somebody just because I had the means to do it.

PAYING IT FORWARD

Thirty years ago, I was a traumatized five-year-old for whom violence and abuse were a daily reality. Human depravity wasn't a departure from the norm, it was an assumption that kept you alive. The education system would label me a failure and make sure it was right about me.

Twenty years ago, I was a seriously traumatized 15-year-old, hitting rock bottom for the umpteenth time and contemplating ending my own life. I had uncontrollable rage, fits of paranoia that kept me awake at night, and a creeping depression. The good and evil parts of me warred with themselves in my soul. Going through adolescence on the streets made me feel lost and alone and led to all sorts of self-destructive behaviors.

Ten years ago, I was an unemployed 25-year-old man heading to prison, which would become, for me, the bottom of the bottom. Finally. The chaos of my mind, which had time and again failed to derail me on the path to stability, finally wore me out; there was no fight left in me. Fortunately, the very darkness that imprisoned me would lead me to my liberation.

It took me a long time to appreciate that each mistake, every hardship, came with its own lessons, some good, some bad, but always with the opportunity, or challenge, rather, to overcome my circumstances, to embark down the road of self-discovery, until I found the version of me I wanted to keep, at last. I grappled with a lifetime of forced sacrifices and helpless suffering that left layers and layers of scars. I marveled at the monster I could have become but somehow managed to avoid (or escape) becoming.

But I had struggled hardest with my own analytic, logical brain that demanded order and balance in everything. The part of me that couldn't stop thinking long after the conversation had moved on. The part of me that played devil's advocate rather than commit to a position. It was prison that finally let me release this, and it was living as a social zero outside of prison that allowed me to finally embrace the beliefs and values most important to me.

The guys at my old place were right: Going to prison is a bit like dying. And it was just this dying that created the possibility of rising again. Resurrecting, if you will. A psychological reset button on decades of toxic negativity. You see, I wasn't just dying to the outside world; I was dying to myself. I removed my own ego from the equation of my life, and thus I no longer carried the baggage that, as Mom's boyfriend argued, had been keeping me down.

When I stopped obsessing about myself, I discovered that I had a deep capacity to empathize with others. It was like a sixth sense that allowed me to key into the suffering of others around me. The more I saw others' struggles, the more I realized that my own existence wasn't about me. Rather, all that my eyes had seen, my skin had touched, my ears had heard, and my heart had felt was meant to serve others. Mine was a tale of suffering, yes, but it was also a tale of survival. Where others might have capitulated to a life of hopelessness, I had fought on and overcome.

As I began to rebuild my life and to absorb the warmth and acceptance of my fellow ruggers and Mom's boyfriend, this empathetic part of me came out of hiding. Years ago, I had buried him in a cave for safe keeping because every time I let him out, he seemed to get hurt. In this new life, though, I had fewer people who wanted to hurt me—and fewer people who *could* hurt me. I felt a sense of my own value and of what was really important to me, and the people who had a problem with that were not people I wanted to be around anyway.

Not that this was easy to manage. I had been in Orlando for nearly three months when an old colleague at the collections office contacted me and said they had a job for me if I wanted it. Going back to that job would mean going back to some of the old people and places and habits, but it was also a job I was good at and could make a lot of money doing compared to the small jobs I had down in Florida. Eventually, I decided I knew what I was getting into and thus how to stay on the path I'd chosen, so I accepted the offer and moved back to Massachusetts. By the end of October 2009, I'd been offered a division manager position and asked to assist with an acquisition in Eau Claire, Wisconsin. I'd never been that far west, but the new me was trying not to be afraid of success.

I arrived in Eau Claire feeling more out of my element than I ever had before. It's a midsized, Midwestern city that is over 90% white. While it has plenty to offer, there's a slower pace of life, it's very friendly, and it feels almost small-townish sometimes. Being able to have pleasant conversations with complete strangers and feeling like everyone was ready to help each other out was new to me, but it was an ideal environment to focus on my self-improvement project. If anything, people found my East Coast accent charming and were interested to hear why I left the bustling cities of New England for a quiet Midwestern town like theirs.

A few months in, I met Martha, who became my unofficial guide around town. She introduced me to her friends and invited me to bars and restaurants, helping me develop something of a social life. We became good friends, though she was convinced that I would eventually want things to become romantic and that I would get jealous and possessive. She would sometimes tease me about it to cover up her discomfort, but I swore up and down that I really enjoyed being friends and didn't mind if she talked to other guys and didn't need to know where she was all the time. And it was true. It felt good, in fact, to just enjoy someone's presence and not worry about whether they were making a fool of you.

Ironically, about six months after we met we did start dating. She was still waiting for the other shoe to drop and for me to change into every other man she'd dated, but I didn't want to become that man (again) any more than she really wanted me to, either. And since I'd met her as the new-and-improved Carlos, in some ways it was easier to keep on being the decent guy she knew than to slip back into the old patterns.

Work took some strange turns. A leadership coup back at the headquarters in Mass., led to the break-up of the acquisition plan. They offered to bring me back, but I looked around at my quiet life in my quiet town and declined. Then I teamed up with the guy whose business I had been trying to acquire, as well as another local business owner, to form our own collection agency. It was less than one year since I had been in prison, and here I was a partner in my own business and in a healthy relationship with a wonderful woman. I felt the hand of God protecting and blessing me.

If there was any downside, it was that only a handful of people in my new life really knew my story. Those who knew it did not necessarily appreciate what it meant, how hard it had been for me to get to where I now was. It was not that I felt like I had to hide anything; it was more that it wasn't something that came up at your average night out: "Hey, did you see the Brewers game? Oh, and do you know I have 12 felony arrests and spent four months in a county lock-up? Pass the pretzels."

In another ironic turn of events, I was speaking one day with my friend Emmitt. Even in my street days, I'd been the kind of guy people could talk to and share their problems with. I hadn't buried my empathic self so deep that I couldn't access that side of me at all, I was just careful with it. I'd like to think I was even pretty good at giving advice, even if I wasn't fantastic at following it. So, Emmitt explained how he had been down on his luck. His childhood dream of becoming an NFL player was just that; a dream. He'd spent his rent money on booze, clothes and accessories he couldn't afford and was now couch bumming his way through life directionless, depressed, and defeated. Sound familiar?

"That's tough, man," I consoled him. "But, hey, if you don't know what you want, let's sit down and talk for a bit. We can go over some ideas, figure out your next steps and try to make a plan and get there, you know?"

He scoffed gently. "Thanks, Carlos, but I don't think you really understand how hard this has been for me."

This kind of shocked me, honestly. Emmitt didn't have any reason to know what I'd been through, but it never dawned on me that anybody would think their problems were worse than my own. I mean, I'd been homeless about a dozen times in my life and between juvey and county, I'd had four extended stints behind bars. There weren't many people who had screwed up their lives as badly as I had.

But I didn't get defensive or angry. Instead, I let him into my world. I began to tell him some of the stories I've told here. You have to imagine us at happy hour, still in our polos and khakis from work, and here's one guy telling his buddy that he once stole an SUV and drove it off the freeway or that he stabbed a guy outside of a wings shop. He was astonished and perplexed, but as he began to appreciate what I was telling him, my words of advice grew weightier. I showed him how my past choices had led to negative consequences, then explained how he could go down a similar path or could go in another direction and get his life back together.

"I have to be honest with you, Emmitt," I told him. "The way you're talking ... I've seen this kind of thing before, and I think you're heading down the self-destructive path."

"No way, man," he insisted. "I'm not going to do anything dumb."

"I hope not, but listen: I'm here for you, okay?"

Here's another point where the movie version of my life would have Emmitt deciding to make a change and get back on track, and now Carlos is a hero for helping his friends avoid his mistakes. But that's still not my life. Emmitt went out and did exactly as I thought he would. He had to find his own rock bottom before he could pick himself up, brush himself off, and make a lasting change. I took two things away from this experience with Emmitt, however. First, everything I've been through has made me pretty good at understanding people and how to help them. Second, I don't have to be the savior who fixes everyone's problems. It's enough to speak truth and hope into their lives at whatever point our paths cross and to stand by them as long as they'll let me. I could be a Miss Fox or a Nancy Schwoyer and give people those little hand-holds of faith that can carry them through their own dark times. Years later, Emmitt is doing great, living the life he'd thought had escaped him.

I also started to think about how people approach the idea of change. When people came to me with problems, I realized they didn't all come with the same motivations. Most people wanted a quick solution to an immediate problem. I didn't have much advice for them, because I knew that there were bigger habits of thought and deed that would lead them back to the same problems again. Plenty of people just need to vent and don't really want to talk about solutions at all. Others sink into swamps of guilt and pessimism. Then you have the martyrs, the ones who have heard all the advice and tried all the solutions but cannot change their situation because no one has ever experienced tribulations like theirs in the history of tribulations. I understood that all these people needed a kind ear to receive all their negative energy, but I also knew that until they were willing to do some real reflection, they were not likely to see real change.

For a long time, my observations about human behavior and people's ability to change remained just that: observations. Outside of a surprisingly normal social and romantic life, my work life took several unexpected turns that kept me plenty busy. For starters, my two business partners in the collection agency secretly began to pay themselves more than the agreed upon split, meaning they were short-changing the company's savings and harming our ability to grow as we'd planned. When I confronted them, they basically forced me out.

I hit the ground rolling and jumped back up again, studying for and passing the Life, Property, & Casualty Insurance Exam a couple months later. However, despite passing the test and jumping through the hoops needed to become an agent, I couldn't find a company that would hire a guy with my record. Then I worked odd jobs from cleaning toilets all the way to network marketing. For a while I worked as head bartender at a new upscale restaurant, then I sold roofs for the husband of a friend of my girlfriend's. Marketing, bartending, and sales all played to my strengths of talking to people, building trust, and guiding them to good choices, so I did pretty well at them all; I sold $650,000 in roofs in my first year.

That didn't stop the guy from suddenly firing me (on *Christmas*!). It's a long story that involved me suing him for commissions he owed me and didn't want to pay, for which I won a civil judgment. (Side note: It felt good to be on the right side of the trial dynamic, for a change.) I went on to do more sales and bartending until my girlfriend opened her own barbershop in May of 2017. I had a decent job tending bar, but I quit so I could join her and help her run the business while she did what she was best at.

Maybe for another person this would all feel very stressful, and I'm not going to pretend it was a walk in the park, but I was in such a better place than I'd ever been, and I was in more control of my choices than I was used to. There were tough times and dark times when I got angry with how people treated me, but instead of spiraling into drugs and booze and sex, I remembered who I was and what I wanted, and I relied on Martha and my friends to provide me the emotional support I needed. Sometimes *I* was the guy who just wanted to vent, but they knew how to encourage me and keep me grounded.

Several other important events happened during this period, not the least of which was deciding to write this very book. The more I shared my story with people, the more I heard things like, "Wow, that's so amazing! You should write that down," or "You've been through so much; your story could really inspire other people." Honestly, I can't say I really understood what they meant at the time. My story was just my story. Yes, I fought hard to get where I was, but I'd also screwed up hard to get myself into some of those situations. Much of it had simply happened *to* me, and much of it owed to God preserving me despite myself. But I also knew I liked helping people, and if telling my story could help people, then I'd take my friends' word for it and give it a shot.

It wasn't until about two years into writing my first draft (which clocked in at 100-odd chapters and 130,000 words!) that I finally found the real Why for this book.

Discovering My Why

It was August 2017, and I received a Facebook message from an old acquaintance named Amanda. I'd met her and her boyfriend, Chance, a year and a bit ago while I'd been tending bar, and because of my Boston accent and gregarious personality, they kept asking me questions. When they heard I was writing a book, they ditched their movie plans, ordered more drinks, and cozied up for the Carlos Show. Not long after that she struck up a Facebook friendship with me. Chance had dumped her, and she was taking it hard, and I was one of the people she wanted to reach out to. "I consider you to be a wise man," she had written, "so I was wondering if you could help me."

I did what I could, and we remained online friends even after she moved out of state—with Chance. We messaged a handful of times as her relationship with Chance went through many ups and downs—more downs than ups, it seemed to me—and I could tell that not only was she unhappy, but Chance was making it worse. They both lacked self-awareness, and his selfishness preyed on her insecurities. They weren't the first codependent couple I'd seen, and, as is typical, the one partner gave off the vibe that he would be incapable of living life without her, and she felt a moral duty to stick it out and try to fix him.

Finally, they broke it off for good. Within days, Chance was finding new girls to hang with, while Amanda still felt hurt and wounded from what he'd put her through. The problem now was that they still lived in the same apartment, just as roommates rather than lovers. She knew that I'd been in some dark places, too, and she messaged me asking for help.

We messaged back and forth for a long time. I knew that this would be one of the hardest requests for help I'd ever face because I knew how hard it would be for her to take the steps she needed. It wasn't enough to get away from Chance; she needed to become the kind of person who wouldn't get mixed up with another Chance. In the moment, however, she was in a weak and fragile state, and because it was her nature, she trusted me completely to tell her what to do. Whatever advice I gave her would literally determine the direction of her life for the foreseeable future.

"I want you to understand," I wrote, "that if you do what I tell you, things may get worse before they get better. You may feel like you've hit rock bottom, but if you walk out that door, there may be another bottom."

"I understand. I'm ready. I'll do anything," she replied.

"The only real way out of this, for good, means confronting some dark demons you are not going to like."

"I'm ready. I'll do it. Just tell me what to do."

She couldn't really understand what she was up against, but I vowed to stay by her as she did it. My first advice was to make her take an immediate step to make drastic, instantaneous change; in this case, I told her she had to get out of that apartment no matter what, which she did, finding a friend's couch to sleep on for the short term. Then I tried to help her connect to some sense of hope. It could be God, a "higher power," or just the universe—it didn't matter to me what she called it as long as it gave her something spiritual to cling to when the physical let her down, which it had so often already and would certainly do again.

I was right: Fixing her life wasn't easy. Chance didn't take nicely to losing her share of the rent and tried to strong-arm her, to begin with, and she had to make some tough choices to find a more permanent home that she could afford. Then came the real work of following the threads back to their roots deep in her childhood. We located important moments in her past that made negative or unhelpful imprints on her mind and contributed to her cycle of choosing the wrong guy who gave her new anxieties. We talked them all through, figured out the patterns, and looked for new actions to replace the old ones.

You can imagine it was not pleasant for her, but she held to her part of the bargain and fearlessly confronted everything. I started giving her little tasks or exercises to practice living into the person she wanted to become, and she went right out and tried them. I hit the library and the internet, trying to understand more about the mind and how it functioned. As she began to feel more comfortable making good choices and saw some of the positive consequences in her friendships and work and so on, I dug deeper into my research and reflection to determine what her next step should be.

I found it in the concept of your *gift*. Often when we talk about gifts, we mean abilities we were born with. Since we don't have to work at them, it's easy to undervalue them. There's also a better-than-average chance that someone made fun of you as a child for using your gift and, because it was such an integral part of you, you hid it away. But your gift isn't about how hard you work for it; it's about what you do with it. I had only begun to really embrace and apply my gift of empathy and understanding, but I'd seen the good it could do in people's lives. I'd helped Emmitt, and now I'd been instrumental in Amanda's life, not because I worked hard at empathizing with them but because I chose to give that empathy away. You see, to paraphrase Picasso, *your gift is what you give away*. And by giving it away, you help you and others become more yourselves.

Amanda, I discovered, not only had a love of animals but an innate ability to establish an invisible trust with some of the most squeamish and skittish creatures. Any pet-owner appreciates how that can be a gift. The next question: how to find a career where she could use that gift. As I see it, we spend so much time working that we need to find something that plays to our strengths. Otherwise work is just a burden, and that burden will weigh down the rest of your life. If you're in a career you love, it can create energy and space to better handle other responsibilities and obligations in your life.

So, we researched several fields that involved rescuing or caring for animals. Some she knew she didn't want to do, so we eliminated them. Others she didn't know enough about and would need to study more or try to get an entry-level position and try them out. Eventually, veterinarian rose to the top of the list. Before she could start veterinary school, she applied for AmeriCorps, which had a three-month program that would allow her to work on the weekends and save up some money, would look good on a resume, and might introduce her to people who could open doors for her in the future.

Everything went as planned—which is not something I can often say about my life, but it speaks to the thoughtfulness of this plan as compared to the spur-of-the-moment planning I used to do on the streets. She enjoyed her AmeriCorps experience, which besides giving her hands-on work helping people also got her out of her friend's house for a good part of the day. While she completed her assignment, though, I tried to help prepare her for her return to the real world. Like the story of the Ant and the Grasshopper, nothing is worse than being unprepared for the hard times because we slacked off during the good times.

I also urged her to close the door for good on her relationship with Chance. One of the biggest reasons people keep repeating unhealthy relationship cycles is that they get so tired of fighting it and are so relieved to get out and get a breath of fresh air that they don't really deal with the stuff that led them down that road in the first place. After a brief respite, then, they wind up unconsciously repeating the same actions and can even wind up back in the same abusive relationship. If she didn't let herself feel all the emotions that came with having dated and left Chance, she would always be running from them and never building the fortitude she needed to stand up to the next Chance that came along.

Facing those emotions would also help her feel resolution about this part of her life. It's important to leave zero room for negative emotions like resentment, bitterness, and regret around things like that. At some point, you'll just unload those things on some undeserving person and possibly ruin something good.

We were systematic, addressing one issue at a time and doing what we could to get her through it before moving onto the next thing. Life is rarely so orderly that we could really treat every issue separately, but by targeting the biggest problems first, we created some space for tackling lesser ones. Some of the issues were emotional or behavioral, like learning to say *no* when she didn't want to do something. Other things were environmental, like finally moving into her own place.

One small victory came when an AmeriCorps connection helped her get a job at a public zoo. This allowed her to begin using her gift in a way that also earned an income. While there, she simply shared with her superiors what her larger goals were, and they eventually helped her land a gig as a vet tech at a veterinary clinic. That job in turn opened the door to an even better job at another clinic which included help paying for her schooling.

After a year of working on herself, Amanda was living on her own, working in a field she loved, and enjoying a peace of mind and happiness about her life that she had never known. I'd poured myself into her, and she had been relentless in doing the work she needed to do. As a result, she'd accomplished more in a year than some people could in a decade.

Most importantly, to me, was that she no longer nursed the insecurities and anxieties that had kept her down. Instead, she had seen that she could succeed on her own and had confidence that she could continue to improve herself and grow personally. She even met an amazing new boyfriend at the clinic, who in turn introduced her to a great new set of friends. And I knew that, though she had done the actual work, I had been the one to guide her through it. It wasn't just that I could get my own life together, and it wasn't just that I could see how people like Emmitt would go wrong—I could also help someone else turn her own life around. If I could do it for Amanda, I could do it for others, too.

This was how everything I had been through could be turned to good. It was why I was still alive despite everything, and it was why I was going to finish my book.

CONCLUSION

Many of us will have to die many deaths before finding something really worth living for. We'll hit rock bottom and then blow it up and find a new rock bottom. Others only have to die once or twice to say, "No more; I'm going to take charge of my life." I actually get sad about the people who never experience one of these deaths, because only by losing something we thought was important can we appreciate the things that are truly important.

My story is a long series of deaths and resurrections on a rough road in search of purpose and meaning. That's the funny thing about life: You can't really wish bad things to happen to people, but it's only through the bad things that the best growth comes—just like the splendor of the resurrection plant can only be appreciated after the years of drought.

For most of my life, I was focused on survival by any means necessary, even though survival meant pretty little to me. I nursed the smallest hope that the empathic kid inside me could one day emerge and mature, but most of the time I thought that was a fantasy. It's only by looking back after all this time that I could see some of the qualities in myself that helped me to not only survive but to come out the other end of my misfortunes a better person. I think of them now as persistence, patience, resiliency, consistency, courage, and hope.

Persistence helped me get back up every time life knocked me down. Patience helped me run the marathon towards my present happiness rather than sprint towards the graveyard of shortsighted ambitions. Thanks to resiliency, the punishing blows did not paralyze me but caused me to grow thicker skin. Because of my consistency, I kept gaining three steps despite losing two steps and so moved forward, slowly but surely. With courage I came clean with God and faced down my biggest fears, defeated my darkest demons. And hope was the bright, lonely light that showed me where I was going through it all.

From the time I learned about the resurrection plant in high school, I held onto it as an image not only of survival but of the beauty of life. It is believed these remarkable plants can survive for decades with less than five percent of its optimal water content. That's resiliency and patience. When the resurrection plant uncurls and opens itself up again to the sky, it releases seeds that will quickly become new, hardy roses of Jericho. That's hope. The thing is, to survive in the desert, it enters "stress mode" in which it curls itself into a tight, dry ball. In this form, it can be blown about until it chances upon more water, but it is also closed off to the sun and has halted photosynthesis, the process that helps it to grow.

The analogy to my life was obvious enough. I got blown about and starved for so much of my life, and while in stress mode I could neither grow nor make healthy connections with people. Life dealt me some bad cards, so it wasn't entirely my fault that I was blowing around in the desert, but at some point I began to embrace the hard knocks, wear them like a badge, and blame everyone else while I sabotaged my own life. Because I'm a human being and not a plant, I could finally make a choice to stop being blown about and to find a place where I could get what I needed and become what I dreamed.

But I don't think you have to have been a homeless immigrant kid to know hard times or to experience a spiritual death. We're all resurrection plants of one sort or another. We have all had to sacrifice at some point, suffer at some point, and made choices maybe we weren't proud of just to survive. Some of us adapted and evolved out of that life, while others succumbed to it and are still rolling around out there.

These days, I wake up and pinch myself just to make sure I'm not dreaming. Like, maybe my life is one of those cruel dreams where you receive something you've wanted so bad, but before you can really enjoy it you wake up and find yourself in your same crappy life, still. But it's not a dream. The lonely kid who used to watch the stars through his telescope and dreamed of a life as beautiful as the stars now stays up late just to enjoy the sight of his sleeping fiancée, six-year-old son, and baby daughter.

Unlike at any other time in my life, I feel I have my destiny laid out before me and I know the direction I need to head to fulfill it. I have a Why big enough to drive me there through whatever craziness the future throws at me. I've discovered my gifts and found purpose in my existence. I'm a living example of the power of suggestive thinking; I've harnessed the power of persistence, patience, resiliency, consistency, courage, and hope. I live by three mottos that have really informed my whole life: *Pray for the best but prepare for the worst*, *I will not lose*, and *If not now, When? If not you, Who?* They may not be the most inspiring, but they're mine, and they, along with a bucketful or so of others, have helped me through a lot of times when I felt alone with my problems. I've stopped beating myself up over my past and stopped trying to please everyone else. I have no doubt that the man I'll see in the mirror 10 years from now will be as different from the man I am today as I am now from the me 10 years ago.

I've learned so many things that I wish I could teach people just by saying them, though I know most people will need to learn them the hard way and will need me to be a strong, accepting presence by their side:

- Most people play a bit part in their own lives rather than step up into the role of hero.
- Few things are harder than shattering an illusion you've spent a lifetime perfecting, but no illusion is worth living for.
- We try so hard to live like we think other people want us to live, but we don't realize how unhappy those people are, themselves. Better to live in the way that will realize the potential within us than to copy the lives of the miserable.
- We don't like to admit it, but it feels good to kick ourselves when we're down. Somehow we believe that, if we can only make ourselves feel bad enough, it will somehow save us from the darkness. But it won't. Positive thinking takes work, practice, and discipline, and no one can do it for us.

The truth I often come back to when I hear people's stories is that most of us are socially programmed to see reality in a way that demands we conform to someone else's ideas about who we should be rather than pursue our own gifts and potential. Some people are fed a story that says you have to become a corporate drudge and work in a cubicle to have the life you're supposed to want. I was supposed to wind up dead or in prison for the rest of my life—"the worst criminal you've ever seen." Frankly, living someone else's story about you is my version of Hell.

But some of us, whether by chance or insight or sheer will, break out of this programming and rewrite the story. We refuse to become another statistic that proves to the status quo that they were right all along. The status quo isn't very good at history, after all.

And maybe this is as good a place as any to acknowledge the elephant in the room: Some of you reading this book

Conclusion

have been looking for confirmation of some kind of story that you were programmed with. Maybe it's a story about someone pulling himself up by his bootstraps. Maybe it's a story about a brown street thug who sees the error of his ways and reforms himself. Or a story about how you made all the right choices and my life is more evidence in your favor. Look, I don't want to be part of anybody's effort to justify living an inauthentic life. I didn't bootstrap anything. I had just enough people who could help me get back up when I fell, and I found people and employers who would give me a chance. There are periods of my life, one of which was within the last ten years, which I have not gone into detail about but where my criminal record made my life very difficult. Don't get me started on "paying one's debt to society."

Here's the story I'm telling about myself: Though I have more faults than a beginners' tennis match, I had hope, and I had a willingness to keep trying. I had the capacity to learn and to grow whether anybody else thought so or not. I made mistakes, but God's plan for me didn't require me to make the right choice every step of the way. I got my act together and made something of myself, and now I'm someone with something to offer the world, someone who can leave things a little better than I found them.

I wrote this book for three reasons. First, I wrote it for me. I wanted to tell my story to a world that still finds it difficult to fit me into its boxes. I wanted to achieve something the childhood me would never have imagined achieving. I wanted to prove to myself that I had what it took to be the author of my own story.

Second, I wrote it for both the doubters and the seed-planters. I wanted to show the teachers that didn't believe in me that they were wrong: I could amount to something. I wanted to show the teachers who did believe in me that they were right: I do have something special inside me. I wanted to prove to the world that it didn't know me and didn't know how my story ended: That would be up to me. I wanted to show the world that the drug-dealing, womanizing, brown-skin kid with a rap sheet that they wanted to write off was still worth saving.

Finally, I wrote it for you, the kid growing up in the hood who feels like you're born into a life of endless misery that you're not sure is worth living. You are not alone, you are not worthless, and you can live a good life. I wrote it for the kid living in the burbs or in the fancy neighborhood who is feeling smothered by dysfunction, abuse, or mental illness in your family. I wrote it for the felons and the failures, the criminals and the prisoners, the gangsters, the rebels, the misunderstood, the labeled, the stereotyped, the traumatized—anyone outside of society's definition of "redeemable."

Each and every one of you is more than capable of rewriting your story—beginning today. You have everything it takes to redefine the reality imposed upon you by people who don't understand your true potential. You can choose today as the day you let the old you, the you defined by people's worst assumptions, die in the desert and resurrect as someone who dares to become something great.

If my journey has showed you anything, let it be that, though you may have to travel a rough and treacherous road, you can find true happiness. Let my journey become the exception that breaks the rule, the outlier that renders the statistics meaningless. Allow my story to redefine your perception of reality and inspire you to question the answers you've accepted until now. Use my experience as the excuse you've been waiting for to break away from the misery you've surrendered to up till now, and step into the freedom of a fresh start. Take my life as a sign, a beacon of hope, of what's possible if you find and pursue your purpose.

Real change will require sacrifice. It may be the hardest thing you ever do. But I promise that it will be the best decision you ever make.

EPILOGUE

MOM AND THE BIRTH OF MY SON

If you've been paying attention, then you know the last chapter of my story omits a major character who had been present in every other part of my story: my mother. Our relationship has never been easy; I'm not always sure she is glad she had kids, honestly. Personally, I chalk a lot of it up to her untreated mental health issues. It doesn't excuse the things she did, but it explains a lot of them.

I wish all the parts of my life could have happily-ever-after endings, but I'm trying to be honest, here. Things with Mom have not been easy since I left Orlando. Things had gotten heated while I had been down there, and I could tell that sooner or later she would kick me out, again. Owing to my criminal record, I was having a hard time finding good work in Orlando, so, rather than wind up homeless for the hundredth time, I moved back to Massachusetts and returned to my collections job.

I haven't really spoken with her much since then. I haven't visited. I'm pretty sure she will hate a lot of what is in this book, and all of this makes me very sad, of course. But I can only speak my truth when it comes to how I was raised and our current relationship.

That's not to say that nothing at all has changed. The change has been in me, though, rather than in her. On September 4, 2014, Martha gave birth to our son, Carlos,

Jr. Perhaps miraculously, I had managed to survive years of promiscuity without any other kids; I certainly wasn't in any shape to be a great father during those years. But that day was amazing. I couldn't believe that I was responsible for something so delicate and awkward and soft and perfect.

A couple things happened to me upon becoming a father. First, I felt a strong need to be worthy of the role. I wanted to give my son something to look up to. I wanted to show him how, even in dark times, it was possible to persevere and survive and emerge stronger.

The other change was that I began to understand something of what Mom must have gone through being a single mother raising me on the streets of Hartford and Lowell. As I've seen my son grow, I appreciate more and more the impossible mixture of pride and joy and fear and insecurity that comes with being a parent. I see so many of the things I value about myself in Carlos, Jr., and almost none of the bad traits. I'm sure that if Mom had had a Carlos, Jr., he would have given her a lot less trouble than I did. I'm also sure that if I had had me as a parent like my son does, I could have grown up more like he is, now.

My daughter, on the other hand, though still a baby, seems almost a clone of me. She will be a more difficult child, no doubt. I can accept that I deserve a kid like her; I only hope Martha can forgive me for the parts of her I contributed.

Again, to be clear, I don't excuse the things my mother did to me, regardless of the role of her mental and emotional problems. I do, however, feel so much more grace toward her now that I can appreciate how hard a kid I must have been for her, young as she was and facing the challenges she did. She fought hard to give me a roof and clothes and food and a decent education. I wish she could have given me more emotional support, but, well, nobody's perfect. Perhaps one day we will patch things up and she can meet her grandchildren.

Epilogue

After all, she's my mom. I still love her. How could I not? She is the original resurrection plant, hanging on in the desert until she had enough life-giving water to unfurl her defensive leaves and—for a brief moment—send new life into the world.

THE RESURRECTION PLAN

8 Steps Towards C.H.A.N.G.E

Controlling How Adversity Navigates Growth & Empowerment

Envision A Future Worth Living For
See Past the Negative Perceptions of Your Current Circumstance

Connect To A Source of Hope
Build Belief Around the Optimistic Outlook of Your Vision

Strategize & Execute, Immediately
In Less Than 72hrs, Strategize A Plan & Execute 1 Goal

Create A New Foundation Your Future Can Live On
Remove the Energy Drainers, Time Wasters, And Stress Causers in Your Life

Search & Destroy Toxic Patterns of Living
Create New Patterns of Thinking by Exercising New Cognitive Retraining Techniques

Establish Fundamental Boundaries
Boundaries Are the Invisible Lines Both We and Others Know Not to Cross

Call Upon Your Gifts
Tapping Into Your Gifts Will Unleash the Potential of Your Greatness

Assess and Adjust Then Attempt To Achieve
Assess Your New Life And Adapt To New Challenges—
You're on the Path Towards Greatness

To Learn More Please Visit www.carlosricard.com

ABOUT AUTHOR

Carlos Ricard was born in Caguas, Puerto Rico where he lived until the age of three when he migrated to the United States. From the hood to the woods, he spent most of his life growing up in the streets of New England. Today he's a resident of Eau Claire, WI where he lives with his fiancé Martha Benitez, mother of his three children – Castelo, Camila, and Carlos Jr. and owner of The Dapper Man Barbershop. As an author, public figure, speaker and coach, he continues to broaden the power of his message and influence by writing, directing and producing digital media content through his aptly named company, GTG (Ghetto To Greatness) Media., a GTG Consulting, LLC company. Lately, his work has been featured as a reflection essay published in a University of North Carolina peer reviewed journal for the Dialogues in *Social Justice: An Adult Education Journal* focusing on adult learning and mass incarceration.

For more information, connect with him at:

www.carlosricard.com
www.gtgmediastudios.com
www.facebook.com/IamCarlosRicard
www.instagram.com/da.preachin.rican

www.ingramcontent.com/pod-product-compliance
Lightning Source LLC
LaVergne TN
LVHW091546060526
838200LV00036B/729